U.S. CHESS FEDERATION'S

OFFICIAL RULES OF CHESS

Compiled and Sanctioned by the U.S. Chess Federation

Edited by TIM REDMAN

This book, effective May 1, 1987, supersedes the Official Rules of Chess, *First Edition 1974, Second Edition 1978, edited by Martin E. Morrison*

David McKay Company, Inc.
New York, NY

Dedication

This book is dedicated to the
U.S. Chess Federation volunteer
organizers and tournament
directors; without you our
Federation could not exist!

COPYRIGHT © 1987 BY UNITED STATES CHESS FEDERATION

All rights reserved under International and Pan-American
Copyright Conventions. Published in the United States by
David McKay Company, Inc., a subsidiary of Random
House, Inc., New York, and simultaneously in Canada by
Random House of Canada Limited, Toronto. Distributed by
Random House, Inc., New York.

Library of Congress Cataloging-in-Publication Data

United States Chess Federation.
U.S. Chess Federation's Official rules of chess.

"This book, effective May 1, 1987, supersedes
the Official rules of chess, first edition 1974,
second edition 1978, edited by Martin E. Morrison."
Contains the World Chess Federation's official
rules of chess.
Includes index.
1. Chess—Rules. 2. United States Chess Federation.
I. Redman, Tim. II. World Chess Federation.
III. Title. IV. Title: Official rules of chess.
GV1457.U55   1987   794.1   87-2642
ISBN 0-679-14153-7
ISBN 0-679-14154-5 (pbk.)

First Edition

10 9 8 7 6 5 4 3 2 1

MANUFACTURED IN THE UNITED STATES OF AMERICA

Contents

Preface of the Official Rules of Chess

All the moves of the pieces remain the same but the rules that govern play and the administration of the tournaments that support the U.S. Chess Federation's national structure have undergone major changes within the last decade. Producing a rulebook we could all be proud of as a national federation took the combined efforts of every tournament director in the United States. Their labors of love are the foundation of this text.

A list of all who helped would be a book in itself. USCF, however, is particularly indebted to Bill Abbott (Yucca Valley, CA), Denis Barry (Edison, NJ), Phil Coolidge (Boston, MA), Craig Crenshaw (McLean, VA), Bob Erkes (Baltimore, MD), Bill Goichberg (Mt. Vernon, NY), Clay Kelleher (Portland, OR), Joe Lux (New York, NY), Pat Long (Austin, TX), Ira Riddle (Warminster, PA), Gary Sperling (Staten Island, NY), Larry Paxton (Cincinnati, OH), Ben Nethercot (Topanga, CA), Bill Snead (Amarillo, TX), Mike Zacate (Mokena, IL), and Richard O'Keeffe (Fairfax, VA). Each of these people made special contributions to this text.

Very special appreciation is due Martin Morrison (Hayward, CA) for all his work as the editor of the first two editions of the *Official Rules of Chess,* on which this edition is based. Mr. Morrison set high standards for tournament direction and worked to establish and refine many of our current Swiss pairing rules and other tournament procedures.

My deepest appreciation is given to Jerry Bibuld (Port Chester, NY) and Glenn Petersen (Piscataway, NJ), who wrote the initial drafts of the rules for comment by a pannel of National Tournament Directors. It was their work that really got this text off the ground.

The third part of our composition team was the USCF Policy Board, consisting of Myron Lieberman, Woodrow Harris, Tony Cottell, Jerry Hanken, Harry Sabine, Helen Warren, and myself. We worked as a committee to approve the final edition you now hold in your hands. Harry and Myron in particular spent many hours reading and debating the merits of various rules and procedures.

The final note of thanks goes to International Arbiter Tim Redman (Lima, OH), who combined our many ideas in the current text. He has proved the Policy Board's wisdom in entrusting this task to someone not only with full knowledge about chess rules and procedures, but also with professional editing background. We hope you'll agree that the clarity of his prose provides a good model for his university writing students.

This work represents all our efforts, each of us a volunteer working in our varied ways to promote chess in our corners of this country. As you take your rulebook in hand to begin promoting tournaments, you carry a piece of each of us with you.

E. Steven Doyle
Parsippany, NJ
May, 1986

Editor's Introduction

Eight years have passed since the appearance of the previous edition of the U.S. Chess Federation's rulebook. That fact, by itself, is enough to insure that this, the third edition, will be welcomed by tournament directors and competitive chess players alike. But it has also made the task of updating this book more formidable. Tournament practices in chess change slowly, but they do change. The last eight years have witnessed many revisions in tournament practice, as well as the introduction of a new kind of competitor, the chess playing computer. This edition incorporates all of those changes and even anticipates a few that are forthcoming.

Beyond a mere update, however, this edition includes major changes in structure and content, which, I believe, will increase its usefulness. We have separated the USCF and the FIDE (World Chess Federation) sections for the first time. Although this has meant a certain amount of redundancy, the increased bulk of the book is more than compensated for by an increase in its ease of use. A greatly expanded index will also be of service to both players and directors. Both of these changes will decrease the amount of time readers have to spend flipping through pages to find the rule they know is there.

The FIDE Laws of Chess have been completely revised, and they are reprinted here in their most recent version. Under the leadership of the Chairman of the FIDE Rules Commission, Bozidar Kazic, many of the cumbersome and sometimes outdated interpretations that cluttered the old text have been eliminated; their substantive features, however, have been incorporated into the new laws. The U.S. Chess Federation played an active role in this revision, submitting a draft for debate at the Commission meeting in Manila in 1983, and supporting the draft's adoption by the FIDE Congress in Thessaloniki in 1984.

New sections on sudden-death rules, computer rules, chess for the handicapped, players' rights and responsibilities, the USCF Code of Ethics, and the Crenshaw tables for round-robin tournaments all bring this book up to date with current USCF tournament practice. Improved and clarified time-forfeit and tie-break procedures, along with an extensive tournament director checklist, will be welcomed.

It should be no surprise that a major change in this edition is in the section on the ratings-driven Swiss-system tournament. The United States has led the way in the adoption of the Swiss, which is gradually gaining worldwide acceptance. Our experience with this type of tournament goes back to 1942. That year, George Koltanowski visited Texas and persuaded the Texas Chess Association to try the Swiss, instead of the then prevailing Holland system. Subsequent successes led to the insistence by both USCF Vice-President J.C. Thompson and Koltanowski that the Swiss system be used to run the 1947 U.S. Open in Corpus Christi, Texas. That was the first important tournament to employ the Swiss. Its acceptance, and the development and refinement of the rating system by Kenneth Harkness and Arpad Elo, have been the two major contributions by the U.S. Chess Federation to the promotion and popularization of chess.

This edition further ties the rating system and the Swiss system together in the important area of color allocation. Tournament directors should note that the value of the white pieces has been mathematically defined and related to rating differences, so as to determine the limits of possible transpositions and interchanges permitted to achieve better color balance. This quantifies what heretofore was a discretionary area for the director and should reduce questions about pairings. However, the importance of the change goes beyond merely that.

The Swiss system is a statistical system. By proposing an algorithm that will determine color equalization, we have arrived at a pairing process that can be completely performed by a computer program, without the introduction of subjective factors. In fact, software incorporating this change is currently under development by several programmers. Once in place, it will be a comparatively simple task to run tests to determine statistical answers to the relatively few questions that still remain about the Swiss system, for example, who to drop, who to bring up, and what color to assign in an odd-man group. Our ability to model and run thousands of test tournaments on a computer will soon give us optimal pairing procedures for all situations.

Directors should note that the figure for transpositions and interchanges given in II.6.H is a very rough approximation designed for simplicity of use. More precise figures (themselves approximations) are given in the variation to II.6.H, and I recommend their adoption. The numbers are based upon the USCF rating system and would be different for the FIDE system, with its different K factors.

Any rulebook is the result of extensive collaboration. No one knows better than the U.S. Chess Federation president the number of people and the amount of time it takes to accomplish a project of this magnitude, and Steve Doyle has acknowledged the roles of the many people who contributed their efforts to this edition of the rulebook. Of course they have my thanks, too. I would be remiss, though, if I did not single out the names of four people to whom I owe special thanks.

First, I would like to thank Pearle Mann of Milwaukee. Pearle worked on previous editions of this rulebook, and it was she who suggested the sensible step of including separate sections for USCF and FIDE laws in this edition. But my thanks to her go beyond that and extend back twenty years ago, when she taught me how to direct chess tournaments. One could not have asked for a better teacher, and certainly much of whatever success this book enjoys can be ascribed to her excellent example.

George Cunningham, Professor Emeritus of Mathematics at the University of Maine in Orono, provided valuable technical assistance in defining the relation between the value of proper color allocation and rating-point spread. I knew that by putting the problem to George, I was guaranteed a prompt and accurate answer; in addition, I received his reflections upon related questions that I had not fully considered. This edition has certainly benefited from his help.

I would like to thank USCF President E. Steven Doyle for entrusting me with this task. Although, at first, I had my doubts about the short deadlines that he set for its completion, I have come to see the wisdom of his approach and I think the book has gained from it. By saving time in the preparation of the first draft of this rulebook, we gained time for the process of debate, discussion, and revision that has strengthened this edition.

Finally, I owe a great debt to USCF Executive Director Gerard Dullea. His frequent phone calls during this book's three-month incubation period kept me in good humor and

at my computer. Gerry's many contributions to both design and detail have helped greatly to make this book what
it is.

No edition of the rulebook can ever be definitive. I hope
that this one will serve for its time, aiding the smooth conduct of the thousands of tournaments dedicated each year
to our great game.

Tim Redman
Ohio State University at Lima

TWO NOTES ON LANGUAGE. The manuscript for this edition
was submitted in its first draft using nonsexist language.
After some thought, I had decided that the most equitable
approach to this problem was to alternate female and male
third-person singular pronouns section by section, although it was somewhat awkward. The USCF Policy Board
took exception to this, and to my other suggestion of using
the pronouns they, their, and them in the singular, and in-
sisted that the text be changed back to the traditional
grammatical usage, with the pronouns he, his, and him used
in the generic sense. On another matter, the word "should"
in this book means must or ought, and is used to indicate
duty or propriety. *T.R.*

CHAPTER 1

Official Rules of Chess

I. USCF SECTION

I.1. Introduction

The rules of chess cannot regulate all possible situations that may arise during a game, nor should they. If a case is not covered by the rules, the tournament director can usually reach a correct decision by considering similar cases and applying their principles analogously to the case at hand. The USCF presumes that its tournament directors have the competence, sound judgment, and absolute objectivity needed to arrive at fair and logical solutions to problems not specifically treated by these rules.

I.2. Organization and Membership

A. The organization sponsoring the tournament must be a USCF affiliate. The affiliate may appoint a committee or an individual to handle the physical and financial arrangements. These include such details as finding a playing site, setting a date for the tournament and the hours for the rounds, determining the prize fund and the entry fee, advertising the event, etc. The organizing affiliate is responsible for all financial matters arising from the tournament and must also appoint a chief tournament director whose USCF certification level is appropriate for the kind of tournament that is anticipated.

B. All games must be played in the tournament rooms on the days and at the times designated by the organizers unless the tournament director makes or accepts other arrangements (e.g., a first-round game might be scheduled for play before the start of the tournament).

C. For the inclusive dates of the tournament, each player must be a member in good standing of the USCF, except when such membership is specifically exempted by USCF procedures.

D. Play shall be governed by these USCF rules of chess and by all USCF procedures and policies.

I.3. The Chessboard

A. The game of chess is played by two opponents moving pieces on a square board called a "chessboard."

B. The chessboard is composed of 64 equal squares, 8 squares by 8 squares, alternately light (the white squares) and dark (the black squares).

C. The chessboard is placed between the players in

such a way that the nearer corner to the right of each player is white.

D. The eight vertical rows of squares are called "files."

E. The eight horizontal rows of squares are called "ranks."

F. The lines of squares of the same color, touching from one edge of the board to another, are called "diagonals"; those touching from one corner of the board to another are called "the long diagonals."

I.4. The Pieces

A. At the beginning of the game, one player has 16 light-colored pieces (the white pieces), the other has 16 dark-colored pieces (the black pieces).

B. These pieces are as follows:

a white king, usually indicated by the symbol:

a white queen, usually indicated by the symbol:

two white rooks, usually indicated by the symbol:

two white bishops, usually indicated by the symbol:

two white knights, usually indicated by the symbol:

eight white pawns, usually indicated by the symbol:

a black king, usually indicated by the symbol:

a black queen, usually indicated by the symbol:

two black rooks, usually indicated by the symbol: ♜

two black bishops, usually indicated by the symbol: ♝

two black knights, usually indicated by the symbol: ♞

eight black pawns, usually indicated by the symbol: ♟

C. The initial position of the pieces on the chess-board is as follows:

I.5.   The Right to Move

A. The player with the white pieces begins the game. The players alternate in making one move at a time until the game is over.

B. The player is said to "have the move" when the opponent's move has been completed.

I.6. **The General Definition of the Move**

A. With the exception of castling (I.7.A.2) and promotion of a pawn (I.7.F.4), a move is the transfer of a piece from one square to another square that is either vacant or occupied by an opponent's piece.

B. No piece except the rook (or king) when castling (I.7.A.2) or the knight (I.7.E) may cross a square occupied by another piece.

C. A piece played to a square occupied by an opponent's piece captures it as part of the same move. The captured piece is removed immediately from the chessboard by the player making the capture. (See I.7.F.3 for capturing *en passant.*)

I.7. **The Moves of the Pieces**

A. *The King*

1. Except when castling, the king moves to any adjoining square that is not attacked by an opponent's piece.

2. Castling is a move of the king and either rook, counting as a single move of the king and executed as follows: the king is transferred from its original square two squares toward either rook on the same rank; then that rook is transferred over the king to the square adjacent to the king and on the same rank.

3. If a player, intending to castle, touches the king first, or king and rook at the same time, and it then appears that castling is illegal, the

player may choose either to move his king or to castle on the other side, providing, of course, that castling on that side is legal. If the king has no legal move, the player is free to make any other move he chooses.

4. Castling is illegal
   a. if the king has already moved, or
   b. with a rook that has already moved.

5. Castling is prevented temporarily
   a. if the king's original square, or the square which the king must cross over, or that which it is to occupy is attacked by an opponent's piece, or
   b. if there is any piece between the king and the rook with which it castles.

6. If a player touches the rook first when about to castle, there is no penalty except that if castling is illegal, then the player must move the rook if it may be legally moved.

B. *The Queen.* The queen moves to any square (except as limited by I.6.B) on the file, rank, or diagonals on which it stands.

C. *The Rook.* The rook moves to any square (except as limited by I.6.B) on the file or rank on which it stands.

D. *The Bishop.* The bishop moves to any square (except as limited by I.6.B) on the diagonal(s) on which it stands.

E. *The Knight.* The knight's move is composed of two different steps: first it makes one step of one single square along the rank or file on which it stands, and then, still moving away from the square of departure, one step of one single square on a diagonal. It does not matter if the square of the first step is occupied. This move is sometimes called an "L" move. The knight always moves to a square different in color from that of its starting square.

F. *The Pawn.*

1. The pawn may only move forward.

2. Except when making a capture, it advances from its original square either one or two vacant squares along the file on which it is placed; on subsequent moves it advances one vacant square along the file. When capturing, it advances one square along either of the diagonals on which it stands.

3. A pawn, attacking a square crossed by an opponent's pawn, which has advanced two squares in one move from its original square, may capture the opponent's pawn as though the latter had been moved only one square. This capture may only be made in immediate reply to such an advance and is called an *en passant* ("in passing") capture.

4. On reaching the last rank, a pawn must immediately be exchanged, as part of the same move, for a queen, a rook, a bishop, or a knight of the same color as the pawn, at the player's choice and without taking into account the other pieces still remaining on the chessboard, for example, there may be three rooks, two queens, etc., of the same color on the board at the same time. This exchange of the pawn for another piece is called "promotion," and the effect of the new piece is immediate, that is, it may give check.

5. In a competition, if a new piece is not available, the player must ask for the assistance of the tournament director before making his move. If this request is made and any appreciable delay is foreseen in obtaining the new piece, the tournament director must stop the clocks until the required piece is given to the player having the move. In a large Swiss-System tournament, when a tournament director is not available to assist the player wishing to promote a pawn, both clocks may be stopped by that player until the required piece is in his hand and he is at the board. He or his opponent should then restart his clock. It is common practice, however, to play using an upside-down rook for a second queen. In the absence of the player's announcement to the contrary, an upside-down rook shall be considered a queen.

I.8.   The Completion of the Move

A move is completed—

A. in the case of the transfer of a piece to a vacant square, when the player's hand has released the piece;

B. in the case of a capture, when the captured piece has been removed from the chessboard and the player, having placed his own piece on its new square, has released the piece from his hand;

C. in the case of castling, when the player's hand has released the rook on the square crossed by the king. When the player has released the king from his hand, the move is not yet completed, but the player no longer has the right to make any move other than castling on that side, if this is legal;

D. in the case of the promotion of a pawn, when the pawn has been removed from the chessboard and the player's hand has released the new piece after placing it on the promotion square. If the player has released the pawn that has reached the promotion square from his hand, the move is not yet completed, but the player no longer has the right to play the pawn to another square.

E. When determining whether the prescribed number of moves has been made in the allotted time, the last move is not considered complete until after the player has punched or stopped his clock. This applies to all situations except those governed by I.12.A, I.12.B, I.12.C, and I.12.D.

I.9. The Touched Piece

A. Provided that he first expresses his intention (e.g., saying *"j'adoube,"* or "I adjust"), the player having the move may adjust one or more pieces on their squares.

B. Except for the above case, if the player having the move deliberately touches

1. one or more pieces of the same color, he must move or capture the first piece touched that can be moved or captured; or

2. one of his own pieces and one of his opponent's pieces, he must capture his opponent's piece with his own piece, or, if this is illegal, move or capture the first piece touched that can be moved or captured.

C. If none of the pieces touched has a legal move (or if none of the opponent's pieces touched can be legally captured), the player is free to make any legal move.

D. If a player advances a pawn to the last rank and then touches a piece that is off the board, he is not obligated to promote the pawn to the piece touched until that piece has been released on the appropriate square on the last rank.

E. If a player wishes to claim that his opponent has violated I.9.B, he must do so before he himself touches a piece.

I.10. Illegal Positions

A. If, during a game, it is found that an illegal move was made, the position shall be reinstated to what it was before the illegal move, provided that the illegal move is discovered before both players have made 10 additional moves. The game shall then continue by applying the rules of I.9 to the move replacing the illegal move. If the position cannot be reinstated, then the game shall be annulled and a new game played. However, if the tournament director rules that not enough time remains to complete a game that must be replayed, then he may take whatever action he thinks appropriate.

B. If during a game one or more pieces have been accidentally displaced and incorrectly replaced, then the displacement shall be treated as an illegal move. If, during the course of a move, a player inadvertently knocks over a piece or several pieces, he must not stop his clock until the position has been reestablished.

C. If after an adjournment the position is incorrectly set up, then the position as it was on adjournment must be set up again and the game continued, subject to the provisions of I.10.A (the ten-move rule).

D. If during a game it is found that the initial position of the pieces was incorrect, then the game shall be annulled and a new game played, subject to the provisions of I.10.A (the ten-move rule).

E. If before the completion of black's 10th move it is found that the game began with colors reversed, then the game shall be annulled and a new game played. If the discrepancy is discovered afterward, the game shall continue.

F. If during a game it is found that the board has been placed contrary to I.3, then the position reached shall be transferred to a board correctly placed and the game continued.

G. A director who witnesses an illegal move being made shall require the player to replace that move with a legal one in accordance with I.9.

H. Spectators who are not directors or deputies are not to point out irregularities unless requested to do so by the tournament director.

I.11. Check

A. The king is in check when the square it occupies is attacked by one or two of the opponent's pieces; in this case, the latter is or are said to be "checking the king." Check is parried by capturing the opposing piece, interposing one of the player's own pieces between the checking piece and the king (as long as the checking piece isn't a knight), or by a king move.

B. Check must be parried by the move immediately following. If the check cannot be parried, the king is said to be "checkmated" (see I.12).

C. A piece blocking a check to the king of its own color can itself give check to the enemy king.

D. Declaring a check is not obligatory.

I.12.   The Completed Game

A. The game is won by the player who has mated his opponent's king, provided that the mating move was legal. This immediately ends the game.

B. The game is won by the player whose opponent resigns. This immediately ends the game. Stopping both clocks or tipping over the king are commonly considered resignations. If a player stops both clocks, he should make clear to his opponent whether he is resigning or summoning a director to make a ruling.

C. The game is drawn when the king of the player who has the move is not in check and the player cannot make any legal move. The king is then said to be "stalemated." Provided that the stalemating move was legal, it immediately ends the game.

D. The game is drawn upon agreement between the two players. This immediately ends the game. A proposal of a draw should be made by a player only at the moment when he has just moved his piece. On then proposing a draw, the player starts the clock of his opponent. The latter may accept the proposal, or may reject it either orally or by completing a move; in the interval, the player who made the proposal cannot withdraw it. If a player proposes a draw while the opponent's clock is running, the opponent may agree to the draw or reject the offer. A player who offers a draw in this manner, however, should be warned by the tournament director (I.17.A.4).

E. It is unethical and unsporting to agree to a draw before a serious contest has begun. The same is true of all agreements to prearrange game results (see I.17.C). In case of clear violations of the moral principles of the game, the tournament director should impose penalties at his discretion.

F. The game is drawn upon a claim by the player having the move, when the same position

    1. is about to appear, or

    2. has just appeared for the third time, the same player having the move each time. The position is considered the same if pieces of the same kind and color occupy the same squares and if the possible moves of all the pieces are the same, including the right to castle or to take a pawn *en passant*.

G. The player claiming the draw under I.12.F first declares to the tournament director his intention of making the move and writes it on his score sheet. If a player completes a move without having claimed a draw, but has not yet stopped his clock, he retains the right to claim a draw under I.12.F. Once he has stopped his clock, he loses the right to claim a draw. This right is restored to him, however, if the same position appears again, with the same player having the move.

H. If a player claims a draw under the provisions of I.12.F and I.12.G, the tournament director (or, in the absence of the tournament director, the player) must stop the clock while the claim is being investigated.

1. If the claim is found to be correct, the game is drawn.

2. If the claim is found to be incorrect, the tournament director shall add five minutes to the claimant's used time. If this results in the claimant having overstepped the time limit, his game will be declared lost, subject to the provisions of I.12.L. Otherwise, the game will continue, and the player who has indicated a move according to I.12.G must complete this move.

3. A player who has made a claim cannot withdraw it.

I. The game is drawn when one of the following endings arises, where the possibility of a win is excluded for either side:

1. king against king,

2. king against king with bishop or knight, or

3. king and bishop against king and bishop, with both bishops on diagonals of the same color.

J. The game is drawn when the player having the

move claims a draw and demonstrates that at least the last 50 consecutive moves have been made by each side without any piece being captured or any pawn moved. The number of 50 moves can be increased for certain positions, provided that this increase in number and these positions have been clearly established (see Section K, following, for a list).

K. The tournament director may announce that the 50 moves mentioned in I.12.J will be extended to 100 moves for the following positions:

1. king, rook, and bishop against king and rook;

2. king and two knights against king and pawn if the following conditions are met:
   a. the pawn is safely blocked by the knight and
   b. the pawn is not further advanced than, for black: a4, b6, c5, d4, e4, f5, g6, or h4; for white: a5, b3, c4, d5, e5, f4, g3, or h5 (see Chapter 7 for an explanation of notations);

3. king, rook, and pawn against king, bishop, and pawn, if:
   a. white has a pawn at a2, black has a pawn at a3, and a black-squared bishop, or
   b. white has a pawn at h2, black has a pawn at h3, and a white-squared bishop, or
   c. conditions of a or b with colors reversed and, therefore, a black pawn at h7 or a7 and white having a pawn at h6 with a black-squared bishop or at a6 with a white-squared bishop;

4. king and two bishops against king and knight.

L. The game is lost by the player who has not completed the prescribed number of moves in the allotted time.

1. Only the tournament director and the players in the game involved may concern themselves with the fall of the flag. Spectators, including players of other games, who point out the fall of a flag in any manner may be disciplined by the tournament director to the point of expulsion from the playing hall, loss of their own game, or expulsion from the tournament.

2. Whenever possible, a director should be present at any game in which a player is in time trouble, in order that he may observe the players and take immediate action if a claim of a win on time is made by one of the players. Under this standard USCF procedure, a director must never initiate a time-forfeit win without a player's first having made a claim.

3. If the player whose flag has fallen accepts the claim, the game is over.

4. When the player does not accept the claim—
   a. If a director is present, he stops both clocks and rules on whether or not the player has lost the game according to the procedures in this rule.
   b. If the tournament director is not present when the claim is made, the claimant should stop both clocks and summon a director to the board for the necessary ruling. Play in the game ceases and neither player is permitted to fill in any previous moves missing from his score sheet.

c. The director will uphold the claim of a time-forfeit win if the claimant demonstrates from a complete (see d below) and accurate (see e below) score sheet that the requisite number of moves has not been made in the time allowed.

d. Unless otherwise announced by the director at the start of the tournament, a complete score sheet is defined as one that has no more than three missing or incomplete move pairs (consecutive moves, white and black or black and white). The absence of three consecutive moves, white-black-white for example, counts as two incomplete move pairs. If either side's move is omitted, a move pair is counted as incomplete. The common error of omitting one move by one player and subsequently putting moves in the wrong columns counts as only one error. Moves recorded only with checkmarks are counted as missing moves.

e. A reasonably accurate score sheet is defined as one that the director considers playable. Minor ambiguities in scorekeeping or errors involving no more than one symbol are of no consequence. Indecipherable notations count as missing moves, so that a player may not have more than three erroneous or missing move pairs and retain a right to claim a win on time, unless the director has announced a more liberal policy.

f. The director may use the opponent's score sheet to determine that the requisite number of moves has been made and that the claimant's score sheet is in error. The director may also use the opponent's score sheet to determine the playability of the claimant's score sheet. A player, however, may never be forfeited solely on the evidence of his own score sheet; corroborating information must be obtainable from the opponent's score sheet.

g. If the director rules that the time-forfeit claim is valid, the game is over.

h. If the director rules that the time-forfeit claim is not valid, five minutes will be added to the claimant's elapsed time and the game will continue as though the next time-control period had commenced. No further claims of a win on time from the previous time control are permitted. No player will be forfeited on time as a result of this five-minute penalty.

i. A similar situation arises when both players agree that a sufficient number of moves has been made, but when it is impossible to establish the exact number that have been made. In such cases, the players are obligated to meet the conditions of the subsequent time control, and no further claims on the previous control are permitted. Players must diagram the position to serve as a reference point for any future time-forfeit claims (see I.13.F).

j. A player whose own time has expired may not initiate a time-forfeit claim against his opponent.

5. Any variations on the foregoing procedures, such as the use of the FIDE time-control procedures (with a director or a deputy required

to be present at each board) must be clearly announced by the tournament director before the start of the tournament.

VARIATION: After glancing at both score sheets to ascertain that a forefeit claim is reasonable, the director shall require the player whose flag has fallen to demonstrate why he should not lose the game on time, that is, to demonstrate that the required number of moves must have been made in order to have reached the position on the board. This variation, however, still requires the claimant to have a reasonably accurate score sheet, as no player may be forfeited solely on the evidence of his own score sheet.

M. The game is lost if the player(s) arrive(s) at the chessboard more than one hour late for the beginning of the game or for the resumption of an adjourned game, or after the expiration of the first time-control period, whichever comes sooner. The time of delay is counted from the actual start of the session. However, in the case of the adjourned game, if the player who made the sealed move is the late player, the game is decided otherwise if:

1. the absent player has won the game by virtue of the fact that the sealed move produces checkmate; or

2. the absent player has produced a drawn game by virtue of the fact that the sealed move is a stalemate, or if one of the positions in I.12.I has arisen as a consequence of the sealed move; or

3. the player present at the chessboard has lost the game according to I.12.L by exceeding his time limit.

If the tournament director has information that a player is unavoidably delayed, he may, at his discretion, waive the one-hour forfeit rule.

N. A player who does not notify the tournament director well in advance that he will be unable to play in any round, and then defaults the game by not appearing within one hour after the starting time of the playing session at the assigned board, may be fined a sum up to the amount of the entry fee, payable to the sponsoring organization. The player may be barred by the sponsoring organization from any of its tournaments until the fine is paid. The player will not be allowed to continue play in the tournament, unless the tournament director believes he has a reasonable excuse.

O. The game is lost by a player who has sealed a move the real significance of which is impossible to establish, or who has sealed an illegal move. However, if the director feels there are two or more reasonable interpretations of an ambiguous sealed move, he may allow the sealer's opponent to choose between the possibilities, and the sealer's opponent's clock will run while he makes this decision.

P. The game is lost by a player who refuses to comply with the rules. If both players refuse to comply with the rules, then the game shall be declared lost by both players.

I.I3.   The Recording of Games

A. In the course of play each player is required to record the game (his own moves and those of his opponent), move after move, as clearly and legibly as possible, in algebraic, descriptive, or computer notation, on the score sheet prescribed for the competition. The player may first make his move, then write it on his score sheet, or vice versa. (See Chapter 7 for an explanation of these notation systems.)

B. If a player has less than five minutes on his clock until the time control, he is not obliged to meet the requirements of I.13.A. Upon making the time control, the player must immediately complete his record of the game by filling in the omitted moves.

C. If, during the course of a game, a player has not kept up his score, and declares that he cannot complete his score sheet without consulting that of his opponent, he shall request that score sheet from the tournament director. The director will determine whether the score sheet can be completed before time control without inconveniencing the other player. The opponent cannot refuse his score sheet because all score sheets belong to the organizers and the reconstruction will be made on his opponent's time. In all other cases the score sheets can be completed only after time control.

D. If, after time control, one player alone has to complete his score sheet, he must do so before making another move, and with his clock running if his opponent has moved. If necessary, another set and board may be used.

E. If, after time control, both players need to complete their score sheets, both clocks will be stopped until both score sheets are completed, if necessary with the help of an additional chessboard and pieces.

F. If it is impossible to reconstruct the moves as prescribed above, the game shall continue. The players shall make a clear diagram of the position reached and the next move played will be considered the first one of the following time control.

G. When a game is completed, the result must be immediately reported to the tournament director in the manner he prescribes. Both players are responsible for registering the result. If they do not, they may be fined $5 and/or not be paired for the following round.

H. The score sheets of all games in a tournament are the property of the sponsoring organization. If the organizer requires that a copy of each game score be submitted by the players, score sheets must be provided.

I.14. The Chess Clock

A. Each player must make a certain number of moves in an allotted period of time, both factors being specified in advance. When both players complete the required number of moves in the allotted time, a new period begins. The time saved by a player during one period accumulates and is added to his available time for the next period. Sudden-death time controls are a variation of this, and are explained in Chapter 4.

B. The duration of the first time-control period must be at least one half hour for each player. The U.S. Chess Federation office maintains a list (obtained by writing to the USCF) of the currently allowable time limits for different types of tournaments.

C. The standard timer is a mechanical apparatus consisting of two clocks that tell time by means of hands moving on a dial (analog clocks). Other types of clocks, such as digital, may be used, but only with the approval of both players. See Chapter 8, "Equipment Standards," for further discussion of clocks.

D. Control of each player's time is effected by means of a clock equipped with a flag (or other special device) used to signal the end of the hour. Some digital clocks, for example, have a beep or a display of all zeroes to indicate the end of a control. The flag is considered to have fallen when a claim to that effect has been made by either player.

E. In the absence of an evident defect, the falling of a clock's flag and the time on the clock indicate the moment at which the player's time-control period expires. By way of example, a clock has a defect if the flag falls while there is still a clear white space between the minute hand and the left edge of the mark at the number 12 on the clock's face.

F. When any secondary time-control period is less than one hour, at the conclusion of the preceding time-control period both clocks should be reset by moving them forward one hour minus the time of the secondary period. In such cases, if the players are to be allowed to reset the clocks themselves, the tournament director should specify the procedure to be used at the beginning of the first round.

G. At the time determined for the start of the game, the clock of the player who has the white pieces is started. During the game, each of the players, having made his move, stops his own clock and starts that of his opponent. If the player with the black pieces is late, white may either make his first move and punch his clock or start the clock of his opponent without making a move.

H. The tournament director may stipulate before play the direction that the clocks are to face. In the absence of this, or in the absence of another agreement by both players, the player with the black pieces determines which side of the board the clock is to be on. Mechanical clocks are to be set so that each unit will register six o'clock when the first time-control period expires. It is customary to add an additional minute to each side of a mechanical clock to compensate for minor inaccuracies in the clock's movement.

I. No player may subtract time from a late opponent without starting a clock. A late opponent's clock may not be started until the board and pieces are in place. (If a clock becomes available for a game only after the beginning of the round, the elapsed time from the beginning shall be divided equally between the two players.)

J. With the exception of games rescheduled by the tournament director, all games of the round should start promptly at the time specified. If feasible, the tournament director should give a five-minute warning, and then announce that play must begin. In a tournament where it is impractical for the tournament director to announce that play should start, players should be urged in advance to begin their games promptly. They should also be informed that no permission is needed to start games at the specified time if the pairings have been posted.

K. Every indication given by a clock is considered to be conclusive in the absence of evident defects. A player who wishes to claim any such defect must do so as soon as he himself becomes aware of it. A clock with an obvious defect should be replaced, and the time used by each player up to the time the game was interrupted should be indicated on the new clock as accurately as possible. The tournament director should use his best judgment in determining what times shall be shown on the new clock. If he decides to add to the elapsed time of one or both of the players, he shall leave that player with the greater of either:

1. five minutes to the time control; or

2. at least one minute for each move before the time control.

L. If the game is to be interrupted for some reason beyond the control of the players (for example, in the case of a defective clock), the clocks shall be stopped by the tournament director, or by the players if the tournament director is not available. The tournament director shall also stop the clocks if an illegal move has to be corrected or a draw by threefold occurrence has been claimed.

M. In the case of I.10.A and I.10.C, when it is not possible to determine the time used by each player up to the moment when the irregularity occurred, each player shall be allotted a time proportional to that indicated by the clock when the irregularity was discovered. For example, after black's 30th move it is found that an illegal move was made at the 20th move. For the 30 moves made up to that time, the clock shows 90 minutes elapsed for white and 60 minutes elapsed for black. The tournament director assumes that the times used for each side at the 20th move were proportional to the times used at the 30th move and calculates as follows:

white: 90 minutes x (20 moves/30 moves) = 60 minutes;

black: 60 minutes x (20 moves/30 moves) = 40 minutes.

He would then reset the clocks at 60 minutes for white and 40 minutes for black.

N. A resignation or an agreement to draw remains valid even when it is found later that the flag of one side had fallen.

O. If both flags have fallen virtually at the same time and the tournament director is unable to establish which flag fell first, the game shall continue.

P. The tournament director shall refrain from calling a player's attention to the fact that his opponent has made a move or that he has forgotten to stop his clock after he has made a move.

Q. If a player stops both clocks to summon the director, he should make clear to his opponent that he is not resigning the game.

I.15. The Adjournment of the Game

A. If a game is not finished at the end of the time prescribed for play, the tournament director indicates that it is time for adjournment. At that point the player having the move, after deciding on the move he is to make, does not make that move on the board, but instead writes it in unambiguous notation on his score sheet, puts his score sheet and that of his opponent in the sealed move envelope, seals the envelope, and then stops both clocks. Until he has stopped both clocks, the player retains the right to change his sealed move. If the player, after being told that it is time for adjournment, makes his move on the chessboard, for whatever reason, that move becomes the sealed move. If a player is recording the game in a score book, the tournament director may, at his discretion, either take possession of the entire score book or may allow the sealed move to be written on a separate piece of paper, which is then inserted into the envelope for sealing.

B. In tournaments with only one round being played each day, when the adjournment time is fixed beforehand (normally after the full period of the first time control), a player who has completed the number of moves required may ask the tournament director for permission to seal early. In such a case, the player absorbs the time remaining before the scheduled adjournment by having the tournament director advance his clock by the amount of time remaining in the session. These requests are ordinarily granted during the last hour of the session.

C. The duration of all playing sessions shall be controlled by the wall clock, but the tournament director should refrain from adjourning any game in which one or both players are in serious time trouble. This situation could arise, for example, if the players started late or if their clock ran a little slow.

D. In tournaments with only one round per day, an adjournment session of one additional secondary time-control period may be scheduled for the same day as a round. On a day that would otherwise be "free" for players, adjournment sessions may be scheduled for up to a total of three secondary time-control periods.

E. When more than one round is played in a day, the tournament director may adjourn games at any time after the first time control has been reached, bearing in mind that he should avoid the adjournment of games when a player is in severe time trouble.

F. Upon the envelope shall be indicated:

1. the names of the players,

2. the position immediately before the sealed move,

3. the time used by each player,

4. the name of the player who has sealed the move and the number of that move,

5. the date and the time the game is to be resumed, and

6. the signatures of both players, indicating they verify and understand the information written on the envelope.

G. The tournament director is responsible for custody of the envelope.

H. Permanent adjudications are not normally used in USCF games. If they are to be used in other than emergency situations, this fact must be clearly specified in all written announcements of the tournament and clearly posted and announced orally at the tournament site.

I.16. The Resumption of the Adjourned Game

A. When the game is resumed, the position immediately before the sealed move shall be set up on the chessboard, and the time used by each player when the game was adjourned shall be indicated on the clocks.

B. The envelope shall be opened only when the player who must reply to the sealed move is present. The tournament director then opens the envelope, makes the sealed move on the chessboard, and starts the player's clock.

1. If two players have agreed to a draw and then find, when the envelope has been opened, that an invalid move was sealed, the draw stands.

2. If one of the players resigned and then finds, when the envelope has been opened, that an invalid move was sealed, the resignation stands.

C. If the player having to respond to the sealed move is absent, his clock shall be started but the envelope containing the sealed move shall be opened only when he arrives.

D. If the player who has sealed the move is absent, the player responding to the sealed move is not obliged to play the move on the chessboard. He has the right to record his move in reply on his score sheet, seal it in an envelope, stop his clock, and start his opponent's clock. The envelope should then be given to the tournament director and opened on the opponent's arrival.

E. If the envelope containing the move recorded in accordance with I.15 has disappeared, the game shall be resumed from the position at the time of adjournment with the clock times as they were at the time of adjournment. If it is impossible to reestablish the position, the game is annulled and a new game must be played, unless the tournament director determines it is impractical to do so or another solution offers greater equity. If the time used cannot be reestablished, the tournament director must decide on how to reset the clocks. The player who sealed the move now makes the move on the board.

F. If, upon resumption of the game, the time used has been incorrectly indicated on either clock, and if either player points this out before making a move, the error must be corrected. If the error is not so established, then the game continues without any correction, unless the tournament director decides that the consequences would be too severe.

G. If players agree on the result of an adjourned game before the time specified for its resumption, both players must notify the director.

H. In all tournaments, every effort should be made to complete all unfinished games from previous rounds before the last round begins.

I.17. The Conduct of the Players

A. Prohibitions.

1. During the game, players are forbidden to make use of handwritten, printed, or otherwise recorded matter, or to analyze the game on another chessboard. They are also forbidden to have recourse to the advice or opinion of a third party, whether solicited or not.

2. The use of notes made during the game as an aid to memory is also forbidden, aside from the actual recording of the moves and time on the clocks.

3. No analysis is permitted in the playing room during play or during adjourned sessions.

4. It is forbidden to distract or annoy the opponent in any manner whatsoever.

5. During playing sessions, players with games in progress should not leave the playing room for more than 15 minutes without asking permission of the tournament director.

6. A player who does not wish to continue a lost game may not leave the playing hall without resigning.

7. Players may not use computers to help them during a game in progress.

B. Infractions of these rules may incur penalties, including loss of time on the offender's clock or addition of time to the clock of his opponent, loss of the game, expulsion from the tournament, a fine up to the amount of the entry fee, or other penalties or combinations of penalties.

C. Agreement to fix or throw games for the purpose of manipulating prize money, title norms, ratings, or for any other purpose is illegal and may result in severe sanctions, including revocation of USCF membership. Such agreements include pregame arrangements, in which players agree to ensure a decisive game or agree either before or during a game to split prize money no matter what the result of the game.

I.18. The Tournament Director

A. The tournament director must see that the rules are strictly observed.

1. The chief tournament director is responsible for all play and is bound by the official rules of chess, by USCF tournament rules and pairing rules, and by all USCF procedures and policies.

2. The chief tournament director's duties and powers normally include the following: to appoint assistants, as required, to help in the performance of his duties; to accept and list entries; to establish suitable conditions of play; to familiarize players with the playing facility and other tournament conditions; and to collect scores and report results to the sponsoring organization and the USCF for the official record.

3. The chief director may delegate any of his duties to his assistants, but he is not thereby relieved of responsibility for their performance.

4. The tournament director's intervention in a

chess game shall generally be limited to the
following:

    a. answering rules and procedural questions;

    b. correcting any illegal move he observes;

    c. warning a player about disruptive or un-
       sportsmanlike behavior;

    d. settling disputes, including those regarding
       draws by repetition and time forfeits; and

    e. informing a player about his opponent's
       late arrival or about his opponent's leaving
       the room for an extended period of time.

B. A tournament director must not only have absolute objectivity, but must also be able to de-
vote his full attention to his duties. For this
reason, a tournament director, on principle,
should not be a player in any tournament he di-
rects. However, in club events and others that
do not involve substantial prizes, it is common
practice for the director to be a player as well,
but those who choose this double role should be
especially careful to maintain objectivity.

C. The responsibility of determining whether a
player has made the prescribed number of moves
in the specified time is that of the tournament
director.

D. The tournament director must enforce the decisions he makes in disputes arising during the
course of the competition.

E. A player has the right to call the tournament director to rule upon a point of law, procedure, or
conduct. In all cases in which the director is
called, he must first establish the facts in such a
way that the other games are not disturbed.

F. If the facts are agreed upon, the tournament director should rule as follows:

1. If no penalty is prescribed by the rules and there is no occasion for him to exercise his discretionary power to penalize, then he should direct the players to proceed with play.

2. If a case is clearly covered by a rule that specifies a penalty, the director should enforce that penalty.

3. If an infraction has occurred for which no penalty is prescribed, the tournament director may exercise his discretionary power to penalize.

G. If the facts are not agreed upon, the tournament director should proceed as follows:

1. If the director is satisfied that he has ascertained the facts, he should rule accordingly.

2. If the director is unable to determine the facts to his satisfaction, he must make a ruling that will permit play to continue.

In both of these cases, the director should notify the players of their right to appeal (see I.18.J–S).

H. Unbiased evidence is required to support any claim by a player that his opponent violated a rule.

I. If the tournament director believes that an appeal of his ruling on a point of fact or the exercise of a discretionary power to penalize might be in order, he should advise the player of his right to appeal.

J. A player may appeal any ruling made by the chief director or one of his assistants, provided that the appeal is made promptly, within one half hour. The director may require that the appeal be made in writing.

K. The tournament director may reserve his decision temporarily and direct that play continue before the appeal is heard. In this case, the appellant must continue play "under protest," that is, without prejudice to his appeal, regardless of the outcome of further play. If the player continues a game under protest and wins that game, the appeal will be considered moot.

L. If the chief tournament director believes that the appeal is justified, he may reverse or modify any previous decision made by himself or one of his assistants. If he does not believe that the appeal is justified, he so notifies the appellant and advises him of his right to pursue the appeal further.

M. If a player notifies the tournament director that he desires to pursue the appeal further, the director shall appoint a committee to hear the appeal, unless the orderly progress of the tournament would be disturbed by such action. If the director determines that a committee meeting would disrupt orderly progress of the tournament, then the player may preserve his rights to share in the prize fund by requesting to be paired for future rounds as if his appeal were upheld. The player has a similar right in the case of losing a local appeal but determining to appeal at the national level. Appeals committees (also known as players' committees) are strongly encouraged at all tournaments, so that all players feel that any decisions affecting them are as fair as possible.

N. An appeals committee must consist of three persons, preferably including at least one USCF-certified tournament director. When an appeals committee hears an appeal, all persons except the members of the committee, the tournament director, the appellant, and his opponent shall be excluded from the hearing. Witnesses may be called, but they may appear only to answer questions from the parties concerned, after which they will be dismissed. The tournament director shall furnish the committee with the current edition of the *Official Rules of Chess* and shall call the committee's attention to those portions of the rules that are applicable to the dispute. After this has been done to the satisfaction of the committee, it shall elicit the testimony of witnesses, as it sees fit. In hearing the appeal, the committee must give preeminent weight to the tournament director's testimony as to anything said or done in his presence.

O. After hearing the testimony, the members of the committee shall deliberate among themselves to reach a decision, which shall be put in writing, signed by all the members, and given to the chief tournament director. If the committee finds that the appeal is clearly groundless, it may authorize the director to penalize the player for that reason. The committee may specify the penalty itself, or leave it to the director's discretion. In ruling on an appeal, the committee may exercise all powers accorded to the chief director by the rules and by other USCF procedures.

P. In case of a dispute, the tournament director should make every effort to reach a resolution of the matter by informal, conciliatory means before he resorts to the exercise of his formal discretionary power to penalize.

Q. Tournament directors should realize that the powers given to them under these rules should be used sparingly, to restore equity or to penalize a serious infraction so as to discourage its recurrence. No one's interests are served by what appears to be the arbitrary or high-handed exercise of authority.

R. Any decision of an appeals committee, or any decision by the tournament director when an appeals committee is not appointed, may be appealed to the USCF Rules Committee.

S. Appeals to the USCF Rules Committee must be made in writing and mailed within seven days of the end of the tournament to the USCF office, which will follow the established procedure for dealing with such appeals. A good-faith deposit of $10 must be included with the appeal, to deter frivolous actions, which will be returned if the appeal has serious grounds. The USCF reserves the right to make final decisions concerning the rules and procedures that govern its competitions.

I.19. Scoring

A. For a won game the winner gets one (1) point and the loser zero (0); for a draw each player gets half (½) a point.

B. If there is an odd number of players for a round, one player will receive a one-point (1) bye.

C. For the convenience of players, the tournament director may allow half-point (½) byes for missed rounds. A half-point bye, however, should not be awarded to a prize contender who chooses to withdraw before the last round in an attempt to assure himself half a point in that round. For last-round byes to count toward prize eligibility, arrangements must be made before the start of the second round and notice promptly and prominently posted as to which players will be taking half-point byes in the final round. If a player requests a last-round bye, he may not later withdraw that request.

I.20. Interpretation of the Rules

A. In case of doubt as to the application or interpretation of the rules, the USCF Rules Committee will examine the case in point and render an official decision.

B. The USCF shall maintain a standing Rules Committee of from three to five members to review questions pertaining to the rules of play.

C. All appeals properly made to the USCF National Office shall be referred to the Rules Committee. A copy of any appeal considered by the committee shall first be furnished to the chief tournament director of the tournament involved. He shall respond with a written statement of his own position and any other pertinent documentation. A copy of the decision of the Rules Committee shall be sent to all interested parties.

I.21.   **Validity and Scope of the Rules**

     A.   These rules are binding on all USCF affiliates for all USCF-rated events.

     B.   For FIDE matches, championships, or qualifying events, consult the FIDE laws of chess in Chapter 3.

CHAPTER 2

USCF Tournament Regulations and Guidelines

II. USCF TOURNAMENTS

II.1. Introduction

A player entering a competition has a right to know the rules and conditions governing that competition. What follows, therefore, is an exposition of U.S. tournament procedures as they are now in practice. The most significant features of a tournament should be noted in the advance publicity and posted prominently at the tournament site. These features include such matters as round times, speed of play, major pairing variations, prize fund, and so forth. Players should understand, however, that last-minute circumstances can sometimes force revisions of earlier plans, though conscientious organizers and directors do all they can to avoid changes in announced conditions for competition.

The most common types of USCF-rated tournaments are

the Swiss System and the Round Robin. Rules for their conduct are discussed below.

II.2.   Variations and Exceptions

A. Any variations from these published standards, including variations discussed in this rulebook, must be made known in advance to all competitors.

B. In remarks before the start of the first round, the tournament director should note any changes from standard procedures to be employed in the tournament. Directors should also prepare and distribute copies of their procedures so that no player faces a surprise when the pairings are posted or the prizes are distributed.

II.3.   The Swiss-System Tournament

The Swiss System was invented in Switzerland but was developed and popularized in the United States. It can accommodate a large number of players in a relatively short time and has, therefore, become widespread. Although not as accurate as the Round Robin in determining a winner, the ratings-controlled Swiss is more precise than earlier versions that did not include rating considerations. Its pairings are somewhat complex and novice directors should learn these complexities by working with an experienced director.

A Swiss tournament should ideally have a number of rounds adequate to reduce the number of players with perfect scores to one. This result can be guaranteed by limiting entries to a number no greater than two raised to the power of the number of rounds. For example, a three-round Swiss will produce no more than one perfect score for up to eight players, a four-round Swiss can handle up to sixteen players, a five-round up to thirty-two players, and so on. In practice, however, these numbers are only guides because of the incidence of draws and upsets. A Swiss System, in the hands of an experienced director, can usually produce no more than one perfect score from at least double the theoretical number of players. It cannot, however, guarantee a clear winner.

II.4. Swiss-System Pairings, Basic Rules

A. A player may not be paired against the same opponent more than once in a tournament.

B. Players with equal scores are paired whenever possible.

C. Within score groups, the top half is paired against the bottom half.

D. Players receive alternate and equal colors whenever possible.

II.5. Swiss-System Pairings, Procedures

A. *Pairing Cards.* Before the first round, the tournament director prepares a pairing card for each player, noting the player's name and rating on the card. The cards are then placed in order of rank, from the highest-rated player to the lowest. Some directors put the unrated players, in random order, at the bottom of the group; other directors place the unrated cards above a set rating, such as 1200. The director then numbers the cards, giving the highest-rated player number 1, the second highest number 2, and so on until all the cards are numbered. That

number is the player's "pairing number," which
will be used throughout the tournament. If a
player enters after the numbers have been
assigned, most directors give that player an
intermediary pairing number, such as 12A, for
a player rated below player 12 but above
player 13. The intermediary numbers should not
be used in the final rating report. Other useful information, such as address, USCF
identification number, fees paid, membership
expiration date, etc., may also be recorded on
the pairing card. The USCF sells standardized
pairing cards for Swiss-System tournaments (see
illustration).

B. *Ratings of Players.* The rating entered on a
player's card is his last published USCF rating,
unless use of a particular rating list was specified
in the advance publicity. A foreign entrant
without a USCF rating may be given his most
recent FIDE (international) rating, or, if he has
none, his national rating if it is in a system
equivalent to the USCF system. Entrants
without USCF ratings may be given estimated
ratings by the director. A director may also
assign estimated ratings for unrated players.

C. *The First Round.* The tournament director flips
a coin to decide who will play white on the first
board, the higher- or lower-rated player. After
putting all of the cards in order of rating, the
director then divides the cards into halves,
pairing the highest player in the top half against
the highest player in the bottom half, the second
highest in the top half against the second highest
in the bottom half, alternating colors down
through each half (e.g., if the coin toss deter-

PAIRING NO. _____   RATING _____

Round No.	COLOR W	COLOR B	Opponent No.	Circle if unplayed SCORE GAME	Circle if unplayed SCORE TOTAL	TIE BREAK A	TIE BREAK B
1							
2							
3							
4							
5							
6							
7							
8							

NAME _____

ADDRESS _____

_____

USCF ID No. _____ EXP. DATE _____

OTHER _____

ENTRY FEES $_____   OTHER FEES $ _____

USCF DUES $ _____ OTHER DUES $ _____ TOTAL $ _____

PRIZE: Place _____ AMOUNT $ _____

No. US–12 Swiss Pairing Card (rev. 4/79)
United States Chess Federation, New Windsor, New York 12550

mined that the higher-rated player on board one would receive white, the higher rated on board two would receive black, and so on). If there is an odd number of players in the tournament, the lowest-rated player receives a one-point bye. The boards are numbered in the playing hall, and the pairings are posted on pairing sheets that indicate each player's opponent, board number, and color. It is customary to assign the highest-rated player in the top score group to board one, the second highest in that group to board two, etc. The director may modify the pairings somewhat in the early rounds in order to avoid pairing family members, close friends, or members of the same club against each other.

D. *Late Entrants*. The director may accept and pair entrants after the announced closing time for registration, but the late entrant forfeits any round missed if it is inconvenient or too late to pair the entrant for play. The director may assign a "pairing score," to be used to pair the late player for subsequent rounds (but not to count toward the final score), if he feels that counting each unplayed game as a loss would be unfair to the other players in subsequent rounds by giving the late entrant overly easy opposition. Late entrants may also be given half-point byes (see I.19.C). Late entrants are assigned pairing numbers as described in II.5.A above.

E. *Byes*. In any round, if the total number of players in a tournament or section of a tournament is uneven, one player is given a full-point bye. His score is posted as a win on the wall chart, but circled to indicate that the game was not played. A player must not be given a bye more than once, nor should a full-point bye be given to a late entrant.

In the first round, the bye is given to the player with the lowest USCF rating. In subsequent rounds it is given to the lowest-rated player (if any) in the lowest-score group. Directors should make efforts to ensure that unrated players play at least four games in their first tournament so that they may receive an official rating. If practical, byes should be assigned only to rated players for the first four rounds of an event.

F. *Alternatives to Byes: Variations.* Awarding byes is often necessary to smooth the progress of a tournament, but they deprive a player of an expected game. To avoid this, two variations have come into practice:

1. *The Houseman.* Sometimes a spectator will agree to play a game against a player who would otherwise expect a bye. Care should be taken that this pairing results in a reasonable contest, i.e., that the houseman has a rating approximately within the range of the lowest score group.

2. *Cross-round Pairings.* The player who expects the bye is asked to wait until one of the games in the lowest score groups has finished. The loser of that game is then asked to play the next round game early, after a brief rest. The director then pairs the two players and marks the pairing and the result in the appropriate round boxes for each player: for the player who would have received the bye, in the current round; for the opponent, in the next round. This sometimes has the advantage of eliminating the need for a bye in the following round.

These two variations may be combined.

G. *Scoring*. The tournament director records the results of the games on the pairing cards. These results should also be posted, as quickly as convenient, on wall charts that are prominently displayed (see illustration). If a player fails to appear within one hour of the start of the round, the game is scored as a loss for him and a win for his opponent. That player is then dropped from the tournament, unless he presents an acceptable excuse to the director. His subsequent games are also scored as zero. A player may also withdraw from the tournament, in which case his remaining games are scored as zero.

The scores of unplayed games, including byes,

– CUMULATIVE SCORES AFTER EACH ROUND –

NO.	PLAYER'S FULL NAME — AS SHOWN ON MEMBERSHIP CARD –	RATING	ROUND 1 COL.	OPP.	ROUND 2 COL.	OPP.	ROUND 3 COL.	OPP.	ROUND 4 COL.	OPP.	ROUND 5 COL.	OPP.	ROUND 6 COL.	OPP.	ROUND 7 COL.	OPP.	ROUND 8 COL.	OPP.	
1	Attack, Allen A. ID No. 11111111	2000	B 1	5	W 2	4	B 2	2											2
2	Bishop, Barbara B. ID No. 22222222	1950	W 1	6	B 2	3	W 3	1											3
3	Chesser, Curtis C. ID No. 33333333	1900	B 1	7	W 1	2	B 1½	5											1½
4	Defender, Donald D. ID No. 44444444	1850	W 1	8	B 1	1	W 2	7											2
5	Enpassant, Edwin E. ID No. 55555555	1800	W 0	1	B 1	8	W 1½	3											1½
6	Files, Fred F. ID No. 66666666	1750	B 0	2	W 0	7	B 0	8											0
7	Goodplayer, Gordon G. ID No. 77777777	1700	W 0	3	B 1	6	B 1	4											1
8	Helpmate, Harry H. ID No. 88888888	1650	B 0	4	W 0	5	W 1	6											1
9	ID No.																		
0	ID No.																		

No. US-18 Swiss Tournament Results Chart (rev. 10/77)   UNITED STATES CHESS FEDERATION • NEW WINDSOR, NEW YORK 12550 are circled on the pairing cards, on the wall chart, and on the rating report (if it differs from the wall chart). Unplayed games are not USCF rated.

H. *Unfinished Games.* If at all possible, without imposing unreasonable delay in the start of the next round upon the other players, all games from one round should be finished before the next round is paired. If this is not possible, the director has several options:

1. *Temporary Adjudications.* The director can adjourn the unfinished game(s) and either pair the players as having drawn or, in consultation with strong players whose own pairings are not affected directly or indirectly, pair the players as having won and lost or won and drawn.

2. *The Kashdan System.* The director privately asks each player at adjournment what result he or she is seeking and pairs accordingly. If both players declare that they are playing for a draw, the game is drawn at this point. If a player does not respond, he is paired as a winner. If a player states that he is playing to lose, that is considered to be a resignation. The Kashdan System is generally considered to be the best way to handle this frequent problem.

I. *Accelerated Early-Round Pairings: Variations.* In a tournament where the number of players far exceeds the number two raised to the power of the number of rounds (see II.3 above), the chances of producing a clear winner are decreased. The director has pairing options that in effect "add" an extra round or two to the tournament without any additional games being played.

VARIATION 1. Before the first round, after the cards are numbered and put in order of rank, they are divided in half. The director notes the top number in the lower half and, for the first two rounds, mentally adds one point to the scores of all players ranked above that number, for pairing purposes only. He divides the cards accordingly and pairs normally. The effect, in the first round, is to have the top quarter play the second quarter and the third quarter play the fourth quarter. For the most part, the effect in the second round will be to have the top eighth play the second eighth, the second quarter play the third quarter, and the seventh eighth play the last eighth. This method decreases the number of perfect scores.

VARIATION 2. Before the first round, after the bye, if any, is issued, the pairing cards are arranged in the normal order, highest rated to lowest rated. Then the field is divided from top to bottom into four groups (A, B, C, and D) as close to the same size as possible and paired as follows: In one section, the players in A are paired against the players in B in normal order. In a second section, the players in C are paired against the players in D in normal order. All colors are assigned in the normal fashion.

For the second-round pairings, the players are regrouped as follows: A_1, winners from section A; B_1, other players from section A, players who drew having a temporary 100 points added to their ratings; C_1, players who won or drew in section B, those who drew temporarily having

100 points subtracted from their ratings; and D_1, losers in section B.

Each of these groups is arranged in rating order, including the temporary adjustments for first-round performances. Then each group is paired normally within itself except that if there are more players in B than in C, the extras are added to the top of D, and if there are more players in C than in B, those extras are paired with the top players in D.

In each second-round group, odd men and color assignments are handled as in the basic system. For the third and subsequent rounds, the temporary rating adjustments are ignored, and the pairings are made according to the basic system.

This variation of accelerated pairings produces only about half the number of perfect scores achieved with the basic system and, therefore, increases the likelihood of a single tournament winner.

J. *FIDE Title and FIDE Rating Tournaments: Variation.* In some master tournaments, it is advantageous to make minor variations in normal pairings to maximize the players' opportunities to fulfill the requirements needed to earn international title norms or to gain initial FIDE ratings. The FIDE and the USCF have limits on the permitted flexibility of normal Swiss pairings in these cases, and directors needing details of the methods should request them from the USCF.

II.6. Swiss-System Pairings, Subsequent Rounds

A. *Score Groups and Rank.* The terms "score group" and "group" refer to players having the same score, even if there is only one player within a group. Individual rank is determined first by score (the greater the number of points, the higher the rank within the tournament) and then by rating within a score group (the higher the rating, the higher the rank).

B. *Order of Pairing Score Groups.* In general, the tournament director pairs the groups according to rank, starting with the highest and working down. If games within some score groups are still unfinished shortly before the scheduled start of the next round, the director may wish to modify this order, and pair around the groups with games still going on, taking care to provide for the "odd men." It is often helpful to make a quick table beforehand, listing the different point groups in descending order and the number of players in each group, and drawing arrows to show where players must be dropped (in the case of the odd man) to play someone from the group below.

C. *Method of Pairing Each Score Group.* In the second and subsequent rounds, the players are paired as follows:

1. If there is an even number of players within a group, they are placed in order of rank, divided in half, and the top half is paired against the bottom half, in as close to consecutive order as possible (e.g., in a group with 20 players, the first ranked would play the eleventh ranked, the second the twelfth, and so on).

2. Transpositions are made in the bottom half of the group, in order to avoid pairing players who have already played each other and to give as many players as possible their due

colors. To this end, it is also permissible to make an interchange between the bottom of the top half and the top of the bottom half. Rules on transpositions and interchanges are covered below.

D. *Rules on the Odd Man.*

1. If there is an odd number of players in a score group, the lowest-rated player is ordinarily treated as the odd man and paired with the highest-rated player he has not met in the next-lower group. Care must be taken in doing this that the remaining members of the score group can all be paired with each other, and that the odd man has not played all the members of the next-lower group. In either of these cases, the next lowest-rated player is treated as the odd man. After determining the odd man, the director pairs as above.

2. It is sometimes necessary to jump over an entire score group to find an appropriate opponent for an odd man. For example, group 1 has only one player, the only player with a perfect score. He has already played both members of group 2. He must, therefore, play the highest-rated player in group 3 that he has not yet played in the tournament.

   It is occasionally possible that there will be two odd men. In the example above, if both players in group 2 had already met, they would both be odd men. They must be paired with the highest-rated players remaining in group 3 whom they have not played before, the higher-rated player in group 2 with the highest-rated player in group 3, and the lower-rated player in group 2 with the next highest-rated in group 3.

The odd man is normally paired with the highest-rated player he has not met from the next-lower group. It is acceptable to pair him against a somewhat lower-rated player to equalize or alternate colors, but only within the rules for transposition as explained below.

E. *Color Allocation.* The tournament director assigns colors to all players. His objective in a tournament with an even number of rounds is to give white and black the same number of times to as many players as possible. In an event with an odd number of rounds, each player should receive no more than one extra white or black above an even allocation. In addition to his task of equalizing colors, the director, after the first round, tries to alternate colors, by giving as many players as possible their due ("correct" or expected) color, round by round.

F. *First-Round Colors.* In the first round, when the top half of the field plays the bottom half, the director assigns the color to the odd-numbered players in the top half by lot (e.g., by flipping a coin). The opposite color is given to all the even-numbered players in the top half. This initial assignment by lot governs all further color allocation, except in the last round variation noted below. (A player who correctly guesses the result of the toss gets white, not his choice of color.)

G. *Last-Round Color Allocation: Variation.* In the last round of a tournament, the tournament director may choose to let opponents with equal entitlement to colors choose their own colors by lot, but only after making all the pairings necessary to come closer to equalized and alternate allocations. For example, if after four rounds both players had received WBWB, for the fifth and final round the director might choose to let the players toss a coin for colors, rather than assign them automatically by using one of the procedures outlined below. If this system is adopted, it must be used for all such cases, without exception.

H. *The Value of Colors and the Value of Ratings.* Correct Swiss pairings are determined by the ratings of the players, so a tournament director should exercise care not to unduly distort the natural or normal pairings while seeking the desirable goals of equalizing and alternating color allocations. Transpositions and interchanges should, therefore, be limited to players rated within 100 points of each other.

VARIATION: Tournament directors who wish to achieve even more precise pairings with some supporting mathematical and statistical theory may limit transpositions and interchanges to an 80-point difference between the players involved, if they are rated under 2100. For players rated 2100–2399, the limit should be reduced to 60 points; for players rated 2400 or higher, the limit should be 40 points.

I. *Due Colors in Succeeding Rounds.* As many players as possible are given their due colors in each succeeding round, so long as the pairings conform to the basic Swiss-System laws. Equalization of colors takes priority over alternation of colors. For example, if a player with WWB in the first three rounds was scheduled to play a player with BBW, the second player would receive white and the first would receive black.

J. *Equalization, Alternation, and Priority of Color.*
As many players as possible are given the color
that equalizes the number of times they have
played as white and as black. After that the director takes into consideration that as many
players as possible are given alternate colors to
those they had the previous round. These are
called the "due" colors. When it is necessary to
pair two players who are each due the same
color, the higher-ranked player has priority in
receiving the due color. When each of these
players has the same score in the tournament,
the higher-ranked player is the higher rated.
When the tournament scores are unequal, priority goes to the player with the higher score in the
tournament.

VARIATION: For players above the median
tournament score, priority for color alternation
goes to the higher-rated player; for players below the median tournament score, this priority
goes to the lower-rated player. The idea is to
maintain better color options in later rounds as
the number of very high and very low scores di-
minishes, assuming that the rating system is a
good predictor of a game's result.

K. *Color Priority: Variation.* When all or almost all
the players in a score group are due the same
color for equalization or alternation, the top half
of the group may be alternated, the first player
receiving his due color, the second not, the third
his due, the fourth not, to minimize color problems in the next round if this top half wins, as it
is expected to do. For example, if there are six
perfect scorers, all due for white, this variation

would pair 1(W) vs. 4(B), 2 (B) vs. 5(W), and 3(W) vs. 6(B).

L. *Color Priority: Variation.* With the same idea in mind as the variation above, the following, more extensive variation has been tried with success:

1. When two players within a score group are both due the same color, the higher-rated player receives his due color. If several such situations exist within the group, the first higher-rated player receives his due color, the second does not, the third does, and so on, alternating entitlement from higher- to lower-rated player. This applies to both equalizing and alternating colors.

2. There is some evidence to suggest that this system maximizes the chances for equalizing and alternating colors for as many players as possible, as quickly as possible.

M. *Colors in a Series.* Inevitably, some players will have to play the same color in two successive rounds. Under no circumstance should a player be assigned the same color in three successive rounds.

N. *Transpositions and Interchanges, Some Examples.* A transposition is the practice of changing the order of pairing cards within the bottom half of the group to improve equalization and alternation of color. An interchange involves transposing a player from the bottom of the top half with a player from the top of the bottom half to improve equalization and alternation of color.

Example 1

2319 WBWB	1979 BWBW
2278 BWBW	1951 BWBW
2252 BWBW	1923 BWBW
2199 WBWB	1896 BWBW
2178 WBWB	1825 WBWB

In the top half, three players are due for white, two for black; and in the bottom half one is due for white and four for black. Pairing 2319(W) against 1979(B) is a natural first step. Pairing 2278(B) against 1825(W) would give proper colors to a second pair, but the transposition involves a 126-point rating shift, which is beyond the recommended limit. The proper pairing is, therefore, 2278(B) vs. 1951(W), as there is no player due white within the 100-point limit. Six players remain to be paired, three expecting white and three black. Moving 1825 up to play 2252 would fix all the remaining colors, and the transposition is within the 100-point limit.

The remaining pairings are 2252(B) vs. 1825(W), 2199(W) vs. 1923(B), and 2178(W) vs. 1896(B). One allowable transposition avoids all but one color problem in a ten-player group.

Example 2

2250 WBW	2180 WBW
2185 BWB	2050 BWB

The transposition of the 2180 and the 2050 would solve the color problems, but it exceeds the allowable rating limits for transpositions. The best solution is an interchange of the 2185 and the 2180 players, producing correct pairings of 2250(B) vs. 2185(W) and 2180(B) vs. 2050(W).

O. *Unplayed Games.* Unplayed games, including byes and forfeits, do not count for color.

P. *Unfinished Games.* Every effort should be made to have all games finished before pairing the last round. If this would unduly delay the start of the last round and inconvenience a large number of people, then last-round pairings can be made and the round begun. In this case, the director must be very watchful of the unfinished games to prevent the results from being arranged to affect the prizes.

Q. *Re-pairing a Round.* Occasionally, a player withdraws at the last minute, as the pairings are being made. The director must then decide if he wants to completely redo the pairings. This should be avoided if it will cause an appreciable delay. One solution is to "ladder" down the pairings. For example, if a player with 2 points withdraws, take his opponent and pair him against a player with 1½ points, take that person's opponent and pair him with a player with 1 point, and so on down until you give someone the bye or pair your initial bye. In doing this the director should attempt to find opponents within the same rating range and due for the same color (see II.6.H).

R. *Class Pairings, Variations.* In some very large tournaments with significant class prizes, class pairings have been used in the last round.

The most common of these simply treats the class as a separate Swiss-System tournament and pairs accordingly. Another system asks the

players to declare before the last round if they
are playing for the class or the open prizes, or if
they are in contention for both. If they choose
to play for the class prize, they are paired against
other people in contention for that prize, and are
not eligible for the open prize. If they choose to
play for the open prize, they are eligible for both
prizes. Another system pairs players within a
rating class who have chance at a class prize
with each other and then treats the rest of the
field normally. These latter two systems are
variations and must be announced in advance.

S. *Recommendations.* Some disparity in color allocation is inevitable in the Swiss System, for the
simple reason that pairings are done by score
group and white wins more games than black.
Tournaments with an even number of rounds
cause the most problems, because when a disparity exists, it is larger. Tournaments with an
odd number of rounds are, therefore, apt to keep
more players happy because it is easier to maintain the expected 3–2 or 4–3 color allocations.

II.7.   The Round-Robin Tournament

This tournament format is also known as "all play all."
Formerly the almost-exclusive format for chess competitions, the Round Robin is now mostly used for important
events where time is not a factor. It is currently used, for
example, in the Men's and Women's U.S. Championship.
Although it is the fairest known tournament format, it cannot accommodate many players and so is reserved in most
cases for prestigious events. A round-robin tournament is
easy to pair. Players are assigned numbers by lot and the
pairings are read from the Crenshaw tables (see Chapter
16). Scoring is the usual one/one-half/zero, except that

players who withdraw before half the scheduled number of rounds are completed shall be scored as not having competed at all (the games completed, however, are to be rated). In that case, the Crenshaw system provides tables for adjustments to equalize colors. In double Round Robins, each player or team plays each of the other players or teams twice, the second time reversing the original color assignment.

Most U.S. players play Round Robins only in their local club championships or in "quads" (short for quadrangular tournaments). These tournaments place the entrants in rating order, from high to low, and then break them into groups of four, with the players with the four highest ratings forming the first group, and so forth down the list. These players then play a Round Robin of three rounds among themselves, following the Crenshaw tables. If the integrity of the registration process is maintained, there is no need to draw further lots for these groups, and the director simply assigns the highest-rated player in the section pairing number 1, and so on. If, however, there is any reason to suspect that there may have been a way to gain a favorable round-robin number by manipulation of the registration process, the tournament director is advised to assign numbers by lot. If, as is frequently the case, the total number of entries is not evenly divisible by four, the director may choose to create a small, three-round, Swiss-style tournament among the lowest 5–7 players, although this can lead to serious pairing problems in the last round unless great care is exercised.

To avoid manipulations for color, the preferred pairing table for quads is as follows:

Round 1: 1–4, 2–3;
Round 2: 3–1; 4–2;
Round 3: 1–2, 3–4 (colors by toss in this round).

II.8. Team Chess

Many varieties of team chess exist in the United States Different leagues, interclub events, and tournaments have somewhat different rules. The concern here is principally for team tournaments, but the points made may have wider applicability.

A. *Individual/Team Tournaments.* As the name suggests, these are not true team tournaments. They are particularly popular as scholastic events because they allow schools to enter any number of players instead of a team with a fixed roster. The tournament is played as a normal Swiss, except that teammates (i.e., players from the same school) are treated as if they had already played each other. The top four or five individual scores of teammates are summed to determine the team's final score.

B. *Team Matches and Tournaments, Player Rankings.* Players on a team are ranked from strongest to weakest, according to rating. Alternates must be lower rated than regular team members. Unrated players must play on lower boards than rated players. If a player is missing from the lineup, lower-rated teammates must move up to fill the chair, so if a team forfeits a game, it is always on the last board. In tournaments, board order must remain the same throughout the event.

C. *Team Tournaments, Team Ratings.* Teams are ranked in order of the average of individual ratings of the regulars, not of the alternates. Unrated players do not affect their team's average rating.

D. *Team Tournaments, Pairing Cards*. Team tournaments use pairing cards similar to those used in individual tournaments, except that there is space to note both match scores and game points. Ideally, a larger pairing card, such as one measuring 5″ × 8″, should be used. The front of the pairing card should contain the team name, the average rating of the team, the round-by-round results of the team, the colors of the team, and the team's opponents. The reverse side should contain the names of the players, their ratings, their USCF identification number, and the name of the team captain, as well as any information about fees and dues paid.

E. *Team Tournaments, Pairing Rules*. Swiss team events should be paired just as individual team events are. Teams are grouped by their match points and then ranked within the group by their ratings. Rules governing color allocations apply to the color received by board 1. If board 1 receives white, for example, so do all his teammates on odd-numbered boards, while his even-numbered teammates play black. Byes, defaults, lateness, and so forth are treated as in individual tournaments. Scoring is based on match points, without regard to the margin of victory. Tie breaking is based on game points first, then other systems may be employed.

F. *Team Tournaments, Wall Charts*. Swiss team events are unique in that two sets of wall charts are needed: team charts to reflect the team results and individual charts to reflect the individual results. These latter charts are needed for tiebreak and rating purposes. They are set up by team so that the highest average-rated team's players would appear as numbers 1, 2, 3, 4, etc., the second highest-rated team's players would then continue the sequence, and so on down to the lowest-rated team's players. Note that a player on a lower-rated team could have the highest individual rating in the tournament, but still be placed far down on the wall charts.

A form that combines individual and team entries on a single wall chart is also a possibility. One such form is available from USCF.

G. *Team Matches and Tournaments, Team Captain.* The role of the team captain is:

1. to see that his team arrives on time for each match;

2. to see that his team plays in the correct board order;

3. to advise his players whether or not to accept or offer a draw;

4. to report the result of the match to the tournament director; and

5. to check the wall charts for accuracy.

II.9. Prizes

A. *Announcement of Prizes.* Prizes to be awarded and the methods used to allocate them must conform to the standards set forth below, unless other methods have been announced in pretournament literature. In all cases, these guidelines apply equally to teams and individual players.

B. *Cash Prizes, Distribution.* No winner should receive more than one cash award for which he is eligible. The award may be one full cash prize (if he is a clear winner), or parts of two or more cash prizes (if he ties with others). Prizes such as "biggest upset," "best game," or "brilliancy" are standard exceptions from this rule.

A clear winner of more than one cash prize must be awarded the greatest prize. Tied winners of place prizes or tied winners (in the same class) of class prizes should be awarded all the cash prizes involved, summed and divided equally, but no more than one cash prize should go into the division for each winner.

If winners of class prizes tie with winners of place prizes, all the cash prizes involved should be summed and divided equally among the tied winners, with no more than one cash prize to go into the pool for each winner, unless the class-prize winner(s) would receive more money by winning or dividing only the class prize(s).

Examples

I. 1st prize = $200
  2d prize = $100
  3d prize = $ 75

Players 1 and 2 score 5–0; players 3, 4, and 5 score 4.5–.5.

  Players 1 and 2 win $150 each (equal shares of 1st and 2d).

  Players 3, 4, and 5 win $25 each˙ (equal shares of 3d).

II. 1st prize = $400
  2d prize = $200
  A prize = $100
  B prize = $ 50

Players 1, 2, 3 score 5–0; players 4, 5 (an A), and 6 (a B) score 4.5–.5.

Players 1, 2, and 3 win $200 each.
Player 4 wins no money.
Player 5 wins $100 (the A prize).
Player 6 wins $50 (the B prize).

III. 1st prize = $250　　1st A = $75
　　 2d prize = $200　　2d A = $50
　　 3d prize = $150　　1st B = $75
　　 4th prize = $100

Players 1 and 2 score 5–0. Players 3, 4, 5, and 6 score 4.5–.5, where 4 and 5 are A players and 6 a B. Player 7 (an A) scores 4–1.

Players 1 and 2 each win $225 (equal shares of $250 + $200).

Players 3, 4, 5, and 6 each win $100 (equal shares of $150 + $100 + $75 + $75).

Player 7 wins $50.

IV. 1st prize = $100
　　 2d prize = $ 75
　　 A prize = $ 50 + clock

Player 1 (Expert) scores 5–0; player 2 (A) scores 4.5–.5; player 3 (A) scores 4–1.

Player 1 wins $100.

Player 2 wins $75 + clock.

Player 3 wins $50.

C. *Cash Prizes, Payment.* An announced class prize must be awarded, even if only one player in that class completes his schedule.

Prizes advertised as guaranteed must be paid promptly and in full.

In tournaments advertising a prize fund of $501 or more, prizes advertised as being based on a certain number of entries are to be paid at a minimum of 50% of the advertised fund. Further, the prize fund is not to be reduced by more than the maximum advance entry fee times the number of players required to make up the difference between the actual number of entries and the advertised based-on attendance (prize fund = advertised fund minus [player shortfall times maximum advance entry fee]). No individual prize may be reduced by more than the proportion of the total prize fund's reduction.

Examples

I. A tournament advertises $1,000 in prizes if 100 players enter and only 30 enter. The organizer is required to pay $500, each prize being half the original projection.

II. A tournament advertises $1,000 in prizes if 100 players enter. The advance entry fee is $12, the door entry fee is $15. Only 90 players enter. The organizer is required to pay at least $880 in prizes, no prize to be less than 88% of the amount originally advertised. The $15 entry fee is irrelevant.

$$x = 1000 - (10 \times 12)$$
$$x = 880$$

The calculation:

If separate based-on goals are announced for different sections of an event, then each section is treated separately. If the based-on goal is announced for any combination of sections, then the sections involved are considered as a group.

D. *Noncash (Indivisible) Prizes.* No player should receive more than one noncash prize, the most valuable to which he is entitled.

If possible, tie breaking should be avoided, but ties may be broken to award trophies or merchandise, to determine which player wins any title at stake or qualifies to advance into another contest, or to serve any purpose other than the award of money prizes.

Two players (teams) tying for a championship are considered cochampions. A trophy or other individual prize (e.g., qualification for a further event) may be awarded on tie breakers as announced in advance.

II.10. Some Notes about Prize Funds

These are recommendations, rather than rules or mandates, but are included as some less experienced organizers may find them useful.

A. *First Prize.* A ratio of about 10:1 between first prize and the entry fee is typical for serious tournaments (as opposed to club events or other tournaments organized to provide fun and experience). This ratio should be even greater in an event designed to attract top players.

B. *Place Prizes and Class Prizes.* When there are apt to be a number of players in a rating class competing in an event, it is frequently the case that some class prize is offered. This should be worth at least as much as the entry fee paid. Generally, place prizes should be substantially higher than class prizes, both to award the relative excellence of the chess played and to avoid distribution problems.

C. *Classes.* A common variation on class prizes is the use of "under-x" prizes, where x is a rating. Note that there is a difference in eligibility for a

Class A prize and an Under–2000 prize, as a B, C, D, or E player could qualify for the latter award. If a prize is intended for a restricted group, it should be named by the class or by both rating boundaries, e.g., 1800–1999.

Note also that many players who are playing in their first USCF tournament, although they are unrated, are by no means beginners. Unrated players should not be eligible for any prize other than place or unrated prizes, e.g., a D/E/ Unrated prize is not recommended.

II.11. Breaking Ties

There is no perfect tie-break system. Each of the various systems now in use has its faults. Where it is necessary to break ties, it is essential that the system has been announced in advance. In some events, especially large ones, practicality—the ease and speed of calculation—is a concern. In other events, where time is not pressing, playoffs provide a better alternative to traditional tie-break systems. Playoffs may sometimes be conducted at a faster rate of time than the tournament pace; even five-minute games have been used.

There are several tie-break systems that provide good and objective methods for directors to break ties in tournaments. Frequently, one tie-break method alone will not break the tie, and it is necessary to go to a secondary and sometimes even a tertiary method before the tie is broken. Thus, at least first and second tie-break systems should be made known in advance of the event, minimally with an oral announcement before the start of the first round. The director should also be ready and willing to explain how the tie-break system works, as time permits.

Different systems will yield different results. But the systems discussed here are not capricious or random. Each seeks to discover the "first among equals," the player who has a somewhat better claim to a prize than those who earned the same score. Which system to choose depends on the nature of the tournament, its traditions, and the specific situations and conditions at hand.

A. *Calculating Tie Breaks for Swiss-System Tournaments.* This section deals with various systems that have been used successfully at all levels of play. For team events, see II.11.C.

Unless announcements to the contrary have been made before the start of the first round, players will expect the following sequence of tie-break systems to be employed as the first three tie breakers. Any variation to be used within the various systems should be announced also. These systems (and some additional ones) are explained in detail following the list: 1. Median/Harkness; 2. Solkoff; and 3. Cumulative.

1. *Median/Harkness.* The Median System (named also for its inventor, Kenneth Harkness) evaluates the strength of a player's opposition by summing the final scores of his opponents and then discarding the highest and lowest of these scores. These scores are adjusted for unplayed games, which count .5 points each, regardless of whether they were byes, forfeits, or simply rounds not played after an opponent withdrew. So an opponent who won his first two games, lost the third, withdrew and did not play rounds four and five would have an adjusted score of 3 points.

The Median system removes the extremes from the data, but it also reduces the number of data points. Thus, it is effective only for longer tournaments with six rounds or more.

The standard Median disregards the top two and the bottom two scores for tournaments of from nine to twelve rounds, and the top three and the bottom three for tournaments of thirteen rounds or longer. The modified Median (Skoff System) makes no adjustments for unplayed games, and discards only the top and bottom scores, regardless of the number of rounds.

2. *Solkoff.* The Solkoff System is just like the Median, except that the highest and lowest opponent scores are included. It is preferable to the Median system in a tournament of fewer than six rounds.

3. *Cumulative.* To determine the cumulative tie-break score for a player, simply add up the cumulative (running) score for each round. For example, if a player's results were win, loss, win, draw, loss, the wall chart would show a round-by-round cumulative score as 1, 1, 2, 2.5, 2.5. The cumulative tie-break total is 9. If another player scored 2.5 with a sequence 1, 2, 2.5, 2.5, 2.5, the tie-break points scored would be 10.5. The latter player's tie breaks are higher because he scored his points earlier and presumably had to compete in higher score groups against tougher opposition for the remainder of the event. This system is ideal for large events as it is very fast and easy to use.

Another advantage is that last-round scores need not be included in calculating cumulative tie-break points, since they have no effect on breaking the tie. One point is subtracted from the sum for each unplayed win or 1-point bye.

Additional systems:

4. *Average Opposition.* This system averages the ratings of players' opponents, the higher tie-break score going to the person who played the most high-rated opponents (on average).

5. *Opposition's Performance.* This method averages the performance ratings of the player's opposition. Performance ratings are calculated by crediting the player with the opponent's rating plus 400 points for a victory, the opponent's rating minus 400 points for a loss, and the opponent's rating for a draw. After the performance rating for each of the tied players' opponents has been calculated, they are averaged.

6. *Opposition's Cumulative Scores.* The cumulative score for each opponent is calculated as above, and then these are added together.

B. *Calculating Tie Breaks for Round-Robin Tournaments.* The most common method is the Sonneborn-Berger System, also known as the partial-score method. For each player in the tie, add the final scores of all the opponents he has defeated and half the final scores of all the opponents he drew. Nothing is added for the games he lost or for unplayed games. If the tie still remains, the results of the games between the players involved in the tie are used.

C. *Calculating Tie Breaks for Team Events.*

 1. *Game (or match) Points.* Since most team events in the United States are scored on match points, the easiest tie break is simply to total the game points earned by the teams involved. If game scoring is primary, the number of matches won is a simple and convincing tie break.

 2. *U.S. Team System.* For each round, the final score of the opposing team is multiplied by the number of points scored against that team. For example, if Team A scores 2.5–1.5 against Team B, which finished the tournament with 3 match points, Team A's tie break for that round is $2.5 \times 3 = 7.5$ for that round.

CHAPTER 3

International (FIDE) Laws of Chess

Preface

The laws of chess cannot, and should not, regulate all possible situations that may arise during a game, nor can they regulate all questions of organization. In most cases not precisely regulated by an article of the laws, one should be able to reach a correct judgment by applying analogies to situations that are discussed in the laws. In most cases one must presuppose that arbiters have the competence, sound judgment and absolute objectivity necessary. A rule too detailed would deprive the arbiter of his freedom of judgment and might prevent him from finding the solution dictated by fairness and logic.

FIDE takes the view that the laws should be as short and

Amended text by FIDE Rules Commission, FIDE Congress, Thessaloniki, 1984, used by permission of FIDE.

as clear as possible and that minor details should be left to the discretion of the arbiter. Each arbiter should have the opportunity, in case of a conflict, to take into account all the factors of the case and should not be bound by too detailed subrules that may not be applicable.

FIDE appeals to all chess federations to accept this view, which is in the interest of all chess players and arbiters. Any chess federation that already operates by or wants to introduce more detailed rules, is perfectly free to do so, provided:

    a. they do not in any way conflict with the official FIDE laws;

    b. they are limited to the territory of the federation in question; and

    c. they are not valid for any FIDE matches, championships or qualifying events.

In the articles of these laws "he" and "his" can refer to "she" and "her."

ARTICLE 1. THE CHESSBOARD

The game of chess is played between two opponents by moving pieces on a square board called a "chessboard."

1.1.   The chessboard is composed of 64 equal squares alternately light (the "white" squares) and dark (the "black" squares).

1.2.   The chessboard is placed between the players in such a way that the near corner square to the right of each player is white.

1.3.   The eight vertical rows of squares are called "files."

1.4.   The eight horizontal rows of squares are called "ranks."

1.5.   The lines of squares of the same color, touching corner to corner, are called "diagonals."

ARTICLE 2. THE PIECES

2.1.   At the beginning of the game, one player has 16 light-colored pieces (the "white" pieces), the other has 16 dark-colored pieces (the "black" pieces).

2.2.   These pieces are as follows:

a white king, usually indicated by the symbol:

a white queen, usually indicated by the symbol:

two white rooks, usually indicated by the symbol:

two white bishops, usually indicated by the symbol:

two white knights, usually indicated by the symbol:

eight white pawns, usually indicated by the symbol:

a black king, usually indicated by the symbol:

a black queen, usually indicated by the symbol:

two black rooks, usually indicated by the symbol:

two black bishops, usually indicated by the symbol:

two black knights, usually indicated by the symbol:

eight black pawns, usually indicated by the symbol:

2.3.   The initial position of the pieces on the chessboard is as follows:

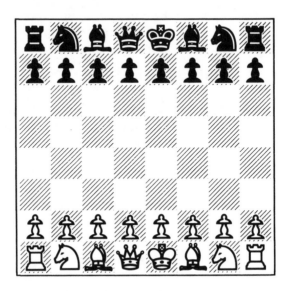

ARTICLE 3. THE RIGHT TO MOVE

3.1.   The player with the white pieces commences the game. The players alternate in making one move at a time until the game is completed.

3.2.   A player is said to "have the move" when his opponent's move has been completed.

ARTICLE 4. THE GENERAL DEFINITION OF THE MOVE

4.1.   With the exception of castling (Article 5.1.b), a move is the transfer of a piece from one square to another square that is either vacant or occupied by an opponent's piece.

4.2.   No piece except the rook when castling (Article 5.1.b) and the knight (Article 5.5) may cross a square occupied by another piece.

4.3.   A piece played to a square occupied by an opponent's piece captures it as part of the same move. The captured piece must be removed immediately from the chessboard by the player making the capture. (See Article 5.6.c for capturing *en passant*.)

ARTICLE 5. THE MOVES OF THE PIECES

5.1.   The King.

    a. Except when castling, the king moves to any adjoining square that is not attacked by an opponent's piece.

    b. Castling is a move of the king and either rook, counting as a single move of the king and executed as follows: the king is transferred from its original square two squares toward either rook on the same rank; then that rook is transferred over the king to the square immediately adjacent to the king and on the same rank.

    c. If a player touches a rook and then his king, he may not castle with that rook and the situation will be governed by Articles 7.2 and 7.3.

    d. If a player, intending to castle, touches the king first or king and rook at the same time, and it then appears that castling is illegal, the player may choose either to move his king or to castle on the other side, provided that castling on that side is legal. If the king has no legal move, the player is free to make any other move he chooses.

e. Castling is illegal—

i. if the king has already been moved, or

ii. with a rook that has already been moved.

f. Castling is prevented for the time being—

i. if the king's original square, or the square which the king must cross over, or that which it is to occupy is attacked by an opponent's piece, or

ii. if there is any piece between the king and the rook with which castling is to be effected.

5.2.   The Queen.

The queen moves to any square (except as limited by Article 4.2) on the file, rank, or diagonals on which it stands.

5.3.   The Rook.

The rook moves to any square (except as limited by Article 4.2) on the file or rank on which it stands.

5.4.   The Bishop.

The bishop moves to any square (except as limited by Article 4.2) on the diagonals on which it stands.

5.5.   The Knight.

The knight's move is composed of two different steps; first, it makes one step of one single square along its rank or file and then, still moving away from the square of departure, one step of one single square on a diagonal. It does not matter if the square of the first step is occupied.

5.6. The Pawn.

a. The pawn may move only forward.

b. Except when making a capture, it advances from its original square either one or two vacant squares along the file on which it is placed, and on subsequent moves it advances one vacant square along the file. When capturing, it advances one square along either of the diagonals on which it stands.

c. A pawn, attacking a square crossed by an opponent's pawn which has been advanced two squares in one move from its original square, may capture this opponent's pawn as though the latter had been moved only one square. This capture may be made only in reply to such an advance and is called an *en passant* capture.

d. On reaching the last rank, a pawn must immediately be exchanged, as part of the same move, for a queen, a rook, a bishop, or a knight of the same color as the pawn, at the player's choice and without taking into account the other pieces still remaining on the chessboard. This exchange of a pawn for another piece is called "promotion" and the effect of the promoted piece is immediate.

e. In a competition, the player must ask for the assistance of the arbiter before making his move if a new piece is not immediately available. If this request is made and any appreciable delay is foreseen in obtaining the new piece, the arbiter must stop both clocks until the required piece is given to the player having the move. If no request is made and the player makes his move and stops his clock without exchanging the promoted pawn for a new piece, he must be given a warning or a disciplinary penalty, such as the advancement of the time on his clock. In any case, the opponent's clock must be set back to the time it registered immediately before the player stopped his clock, the position on the chessboard must be reestablished to what it was before the player moved his pawn, and the clock of the player having the move must be started. The player then must make his move correctly, in the manner specified in Article 5.6.d.

ARTICLE 6. THE COMPLETION OF THE MOVE

A move is completed—

6.1.   in the case of the transfer of a piece to a vacant square, when the player's hand has released the piece.

6.2.   in the case of a capture, when the captured piece has been removed from the chessboard and the player, having placed his own piece on its new square, has released the piece from his hand.

6.3.   in the case of castling, when the player's hand has released the rook on the square crossed by the king. When the player has released the king from his hand, the move is not yet completed, but the player no longer has the right to make any move other than castling on that side, if this is legal.

6.4. in the case of the promotion of a pawn, when the pawn has been removed from the chessboard and the player's hand has released the new piece after placing it on the promotion square. If the player has released from his hand the pawn that has reached the promotion square, the move is not yet completed, but the player no longer has the right to play the pawn to another square.

6.5. When determining whether the prescribed number of moves has been made in the allotted time, the last move is not considered completed until after the player has stopped his clock. This applies to all situations except those governed by Articles 10.1, 10.2, 10.3, and 10.4.

ARTICLE 7. THE TOUCHED PIECE

7.1. Provided that he first expresses his intention (e.g., saying *j'adoube*), the player having the move may adjust one or more pieces on their squares.

7.2. Except for the above case, if the player having the move deliberately touches—

a. one or more pieces of the same color, he must move or capture the first piece touched that can be moved or captured; or

b. one of his own pieces and one of his opponent's pieces, he must capture his opponent's piece with his own piece; or if this is illegal, move or capture the first piece touched that can be moved or captured.

7.3.   If none of the pieces touched has a legal move (or if none of the opponent's pieces touched can legally be captured), the player is free to make any legal move.

7.4.   If a player wishes to claim that his opponent has violated Article 7.2, he must do so before he himself touches a piece.

ARTICLE 8. ILLEGAL POSITIONS

8.1.   If, during a game, it is found that an illegal move was made, the position shall be reinstated to what it was before the illegal move was made. The game shall then continue by applying the rules of Article 7 to the move replacing the illegal move. If the position cannot be reinstated, the game shall be annulled and a new game played.

This applies to all sessions of play and also to a game awaiting a decision by adjudication.

8.2.   If, during a game, one or more pieces have been accidentally displaced and incorrectly replaced, the position before the displacement occurred shall be reinstated and the game shall continue. If the position cannot be reinstated, the game shall be annulled and a new game played.

8.3.   If a player moves and in the course of this inadvertently knocks over a piece or several pieces, he must not stop the clock until the position has been reestablished.

8.4.   If, after an adjournment, the position is incorrectly set up, the position as it was on adjournment must be set up again and the game continued.

8.5. If, during a game, it is found that the initial position of the pieces was incorrect or that the game began with colors reversed, the game shall be annulled and a new game played.

8.6. If, during a game, it is found that the board has been placed contrary to Article 1.2, the position reached shall be transferred to a board correctly placed and the game continued.

ARTICLE 9. CHECK

9.1. The king is in check when the square it occupies is attacked by one or two of the opponent's pieces; in this case the latter is or are said to be "checking the king."

9.2. Check must be parried by the move immediately following. If the check cannot be parried, the king is said to be "checkmated" ("mated"). (See Article 10.1.)

9.3. Declaring a check is not obligatory.

ARTICLE 10. THE COMPLETED GAME

10.1. The game is won by the player who has mated his opponent's king. This immediately ends the game.

10.2. The game is won by the player whose opponent declares he resigns. This immediately ends the game.

10.3. The game is drawn when the king of the player who has the move is not in check and the player cannot make any legal move. The king is then said to be "stalemated." This immediately ends the game.

10.4. The game is drawn upon agreement between the two players. This immediately ends the game.

10.5. The game is drawn, upon a claim by the player having the move, when the same position:

  a. is about to appear; or

  b. has just appeared for the third time, the same player having the move each time. The position is considered the same if pieces of the same kind and color occupy the same squares and if the possible moves of all the pieces are the same, including the right to castle or to take a pawn *en passant*.

10.6. If a player executes a move without having claimed a draw for one of the reasons stated in 10.5, he loses the right to claim a draw; this right is restored to him, however, if the same position appears again, the same player having the move.

10.7. The game is drawn when one of the following endings arises, where the possibility of a win is evidently excluded for either side:

  a. king against king,

  b. king against king with bishop or knight,

  c. king and bishop against king and bishop, with both bishops on diagonals of the same color.

10.8. The game is drawn when a player having the move claims a draw and demonstrates that at least the last 50 consecutive moves have been made by each side without the capture of any piece and without the movement of any pawn. This number of 50 moves can be increased for certain positions, provided that this increase in number and these positions have been clearly established in the laws of chess (Article 10.9).

10.9. The number of 50 moves mentioned in Article 10.8 will be extended to 100 moves for the following positions:

a. king, rook, and bishop against king and rook;

b. king and two knights against king and pawn, if the following conditions are met:

    i. the pawn is safely blocked by a knight;

    ii. the pawn is not further advanced than: for black: a4, b6, c5, d4, e4, f5, g6, or h4; for white: a5, b3, c4, d5, e5, f4, g3, or h5.

c. king, rook, and pawn versus king, bishop, and pawn, if:

    i. white has a pawn at a2, black has a pawn at a3 and a black-squared bishop, or

    ii. white has a pawn at h2, black has a pawn at h3 and a white-squared bishop, or

    iii. conditions of (i) or (ii) with colors reversed and, therefore, a black pawn at h7 or a7 and white having a pawn at h6 (with black-squared bishop) or at a6 (with white-squared bishop).

10.10. A proposal of a draw under the provisions of Article 10.4 may be made by a player only at the moment when he has just moved a piece. On proposing a draw, he starts the clock of his opponent. The latter may accept the proposal, or he may reject it either orally or by completing a move; in the interval the player who has made the proposal cannot withdraw it.

a. If a player proposes a draw while his opponent's clock is running, the opponent may agree to the draw or reject the offer. A player who offers a draw in this manner, however, should be warned by the arbiter (15.1.d).

b. If a player proposes a draw while his own clock is running, the opponent may accept or reject the offer, or he may postpone his decision until after he has seen his opponent's move. In the case where the move is a sealed move, the decision may wait until after the sealed-move envelope has been opened and the move played on the board.

c. In these situations, the player may reject the proposal orally or by completing a move at his first opportunity. In the interval between the offer of a draw and the opponent's response, the player who made the proposal cannot withdraw it.

10.11.1 The right to claim the draw under the provision of Article 10.5 belongs exclusively to a player—

a. who is in a position to make a move leading to such a repetition of the position, if he first declares to the arbiter his intention of making this move, and writes this move on his score sheet; or

b. whose turn it is to reply to a move that has produced the repeated position.

10.11.2. The right to claim a draw before overstepping his time limit also belongs to a player whose opponent has only the king remaining.

10.12. If a player claims a draw under the provisions of Articles 10.8 and 10.11, the arbiter must first stop the clock while the claim is being investigated.

   a. If the claim is found to be correct, the game is drawn.

   b. If the claim is found to be incorrect, the arbiter shall then add five minutes to the claimant's used time. If this means that the claimant has overstepped the time limit, his game will be declared lost. Otherwise, the game will be continued and the player who has indicated a move according to Article 10.11.1a is obliged to execute this move on the chessboard.

   c. A player who has made a claim under this article cannot withdraw the claim.

10.13. The game is lost by a player who has not completed the prescribed number of moves in the allotted time.

10.14. The game is lost by a player who arrives at the chessboard more than one hour late for the beginning of the game or for the resumption of an adjourned game. The time of delay is counted from the start of the session. However, in the case of an adjourned game, if the player who made the sealed move is the late player, the game is decided otherwise if:

   a. the absent player has won the game by virtue of the fact that the sealed move is checkmate; or

b. the absent player has produced a drawn game by virtue of the fact that the sealed move is stalemate, or if one of the positions in 10.7 has arisen as the consequence of the sealed move; or

c. the player present at the chessboard has lost the game according to Article 10.13 by exceeding his time limit.

10.15. The game is lost by a player who has sealed a move, the real significance of which is impossible to establish, or who has sealed an illegal move.

10.16. The game is lost by a player who during the game refuses to comply with the laws. If both players refuse to comply with the laws or if both players arrive at the chessboard more than one hour late, the game shall be declared lost by both players.

ARTICLE 11. THE RECORDING OF GAMES

11.1. In the course of play, each player is required to record the game (his own moves and those of his opponent), move after move, as clearly and legibly as possible in the algebraic notation, on the score sheet prescribed for the competition. It is irrelevant whether the player first makes his move and then writes down the move on his score sheet or vice versa.

11.2. If a player has less than five minutes on his clock until the time control, he is not obliged to meet the requirements of Article 11.1. As soon as the special device (e.g., flag) on the clock indicates the end of his allotted time, the player must immediately complete his record of the game by filling in the moves omitted from his score sheet.

11.3. If both players cannot keep score, the arbiter, or his deputy, must endeavor to be present and keep score. The arbiter must not intervene unless one flag falls, and he should refrain from signaling in any manner to the players that the time control has been reached.

11.4. If Article 11.2 does not apply, and a player refuses to record the game according to Article 11.1, then Article 10.16 should be applied.

11.5. If a player does not refuse to comply with the arbiter's request for a completed score sheet, but declares that he cannot complete his score sheet without consulting his opponent's, the request for this score sheet must be made to the arbiter, who will determine whether the score sheet can be completed before the time control without inconveniencing the other player. The latter cannot refuse his score sheet because the score sheet belongs to the organizers and the reconstruction will be made in his opponent's time. In all other cases the score sheets can be completed only after the time control.

11.6. If, after the time control, one player alone has to complete his score sheet, he will do so before making another move, and with his clock running if his opponent has moved.

11.7. If, after the time control, both players need to complete their score sheets, both clocks will be stopped until the two score sheets are completed, if necessary with the help of a chessboard under the control of the arbiter who should have re-corded the actual game position beforehand.

11.8.   If, in Article 11.6, the arbiter sees that the score sheets alone cannot help in the reconstruction of the game, he will act as in 11.7.

11.9.   If it is impossible to reconstruct the moves as prescribed under Article 11.7, the game shall continue. In this case, the next move played will be considered to be the first one of the following time control.

ARTICLE 12. THE CHESS CLOCK

12.1.   Each player must make a certain number of moves in an allotted period of time, these two factors being specified in advance. The time saved by a player during one period is added to his time available for the next period.

12.2.   Control of each player's time is effected by means of a clock equipped with a flag (or another special device) for this purpose. The flag is considered to have fallen when the arbiter observes the fact, or when the arbiter determines that the allotted time has been exceeded even though the flag, because of a defect, has not fallen when the end of the minute hand has passed the end of the flag. In cases where no arbiter is present, the flag is considered to have fallen when a claim has been made to that effect by a player.

12.3.   At the time determined for the start of the game, the clock of the player who has the white pieces is started. During the game, each of the players, having made his move, stops his own clock and starts his opponent's clock.

12.4.   Every indication given by a clock is considered to be conclusive in the absence of evident defects. A player who wishes to claim any such defect must do so as soon as he himself has become aware of it, but not later than immediately after his flag has fallen at the time control. A clock with an obvious defect should be replaced, and the time used by each player up to the time the game was interrupted should be indicated on the new clock as accurately as possible. The arbiter shall use his best judgment in determining what times shall be shown on the new clock. If the arbiter decides to add time to the clock of one or both of the players, he shall under no circumstances (except as provided for in Article 10.12.b) leave a player with:

a. less than five minutes to the time control; or

b. less than one minute for every move to the time control.

12.5.   If the game needs to be interrupted for some reason for which neither player is responsible, the clocks shall be stopped by the arbiter. This should be done, for example, in the case of an illegal position being corrected, in the case of a defective clock being changed, or if the piece which a player has declared he wishes to exchange for a promoted pawn is not immediately available.

12.6.   In the case of Articles 8.1 and 8.2, when it is not possible to determine the time used by each player up to the moment when the irregularity occurred, each player shall be allotted up to that moment a time proportional to that indicated by the clock when the irregularity was ascertained. For example, after black's 30th move it is found that an irregularity took place at the 20th move. For these 30 moves the clock shows 90 minutes for white and 60 minutes for black, so it is assumed that the times used by the two players for the first 20 moves were as follows:

$$\text{White:} \frac{90 \times 20}{30} = 60 \text{ minutes}$$

$$\text{Black:} \frac{60 \times 20}{30} = 40 \text{ minutes}$$

12.7.   A resignation or an agreement to draw remains valid even when it is found later that the flag had fallen.

12.8.   If both flags have fallen virtually at the same time and the arbiter is unable to establish clearly which flag fell first, the game shall continue.

12.9.   The arbiter shall refrain from calling a player's attention to the fact that his opponent has made a move, or that the player has forgotten to stop his clock after he has made a move, or informing him how many moves he has made, etc.

ARTICLE 13. THE ADJOURNMENT OF THE GAME

13.1.   If a game is not finished at the end of the time prescribed for play, the player having the move must write his move in unambiguous notation on his score sheet, put his score sheet and that of his opponent in an envelope, seal the envelope, and then stop the clocks. Until he has stopped the clocks, the player retains the right to change his sealed move. If the player makes the said move on the chessboard, he must write this same move on his score sheet as his sealed move.

13.2.   Upon the envelope shall be indicated—

a. the names of the players,

b. the position immediately before the sealed move,

c. the time used by each player, and

d. the name of the player who has sealed the move and the number of that move.

13.3.   The arbiter is responsible for the envelope.

ARTICLE 14. THE RESUMPTION OF THE ADJOURNED GAME

14.1.   When the game is resumed, the position immediately before the sealed move shall be set up on the chessboard, and the time used by each player when the game was adjourned shall be indicated on the clocks.

14.2.   The envelope shall be opened only when the player having the move (the player who must reply to the sealed move) is present. The player's clock shall be started after the sealed move has been made on the chessboard.

a. If the two players have in an adjourned game agreed to a draw and announce their decision to the arbiter, and then find, when the envelope is opened, that a move has been sealed that is invalid according to Article 10.15, then the draw stands.

b. If one of the players in an adjourned game notifies the arbiter that he resigns and then finds, when the envelope is opened, that his opponent has sealed a move that is invalid according to Article 10.15, then the resignation is still valid.

14.3. If the player having to respond to the sealed move is absent, his clock shall be started but the envelope containing the sealed move shall be opened only when he arrives.

14.4. If the player who has sealed the move is absent, the player having the move is not obliged to reply to the sealed move on the chessboard. He has the right to record his move in reply on his score sheet, to seal the score sheet in an envelope, to stop his clock, and to start his opponent's clock. The envelope should then be put into safekeeping and opened on the opponent's arrival.

14.5. If the envelope containing the move recorded in accordance with Article 13.1 and Article 13.2 has disappeared—

a. the game shall be resumed from the position at the time of adjournment and with the clock times recorded at the time of adjournment;

b. if it is impossible to reestablish the position the game is annulled and a new game must be played;

c. if the time used at the time of the adjournment cannot be reestablished this question is decided by the arbiter. The player who sealed the move makes it on the board.

14.6. If, upon resumption of the game, the time used has been incorrectly indicated on either clock, and if either player points this out before making his first move, the error must be corrected. If the error is not so established, the game continues without correction unless the arbiter feels that the consequences will be too severe.

14.7. The duration of the adjourned game session shall be controlled by the wall clock with the starting time and finishing time announced in advance.

ARTICLE 15. THE CONDUCT OF THE PLAYERS

15.1. Prohibitions.

a. During play the players are forbidden to make use of handwritten, printed, or otherwise recorded matter, or to analyze the game on another chessboard; they are also forbidden to have recourse to the advice or opinion of a third party, whether solicited or not.

b. The use of notes made during the game as an aid to memory is also forbidden, aside from the actual recording of the moves and the time on the clocks.

c. No analysis is permitted in the playing rooms during play or during adjourned sessions.

d. It is forbidden to distract or annoy the opponent in any manner whatsoever.

15.2. Infractions of the rules indicated in Article 15.1 may incur penalties even to the extent of the loss of the game.

ARTICLE 16. THE ARBITER

An arbiter should be designated to control the competition. His duties are:

16.1. To see that the laws are strictly observed.

16.2. To supervise the progress of the competition, to establish that the prescribed time limit has not been exceeded by the players, to arrange the order of resumption of play of adjourned games, to see that the arrangements contained in Article 13 are observed (to see that the information on the envelope is correct), to keep the sealed-move envelope until the resumption of the adjourned game, etc.

16.3. To enforce the decisions he may make in disputes that have arisen during the course of the competition.

16.4. To act in the best interest of the competition to ensure that a good playing environment is maintained and that the players are not disturbed by each other or by the audience.

16.5. To impose penalties on the players for any fault or infraction of the laws.

ARTICLE 17. SCORING

For a won game the winner gets 1 (one) point and the loser 0 (zero); for a draw each player gets ½ (half a point).

ARTICLE 18. THE INTERPRETATION
OF THE LAWS

In case of doubt as to the application or interpretation of the laws, FIDE will examine the evidence and render official decisions. Rulings published are binding on all affiliated federations. All proposals and questions about interpretations should be submitted by member federations, with complete data.

ARTICLE 19. VALIDITY

This English text is the authentic version of the *Laws of Chess*, which was adopted by the 1984 FIDE Congress. These laws took effect from January 1, 1985.

CHAPTER 4

Sudden-Death Rules

NOTE: A sudden-death time control is a relatively recent addition to tournament procedure. Until such time as players are familiar with these controls, USCF strongly recommends that a copy of these rules be posted whenever a sudden-death control is likely to be in effect.

1. Definition. A sudden-death time control requires each player to make all the moves of the game in a certain period of time, as opposed to more standard time controls that require only a certain number of moves in a given time.

2. Purpose. The purpose of sudden-death time controls is to guarantee that a round will be finished no later than a given time. They are, therefore, particularly useful in situations when the availability of a tournament site is limited in time, or when the players themselves have only limited time available for a tournament.

3. Restrictions. In order to use a sudden-death time control in a tournament:

    A. Advance notice must be given in all *Chess Life* ads and other publicity.

    B. There must be at least 30 minutes per player in a sudden-death time control.

    C. The USCF office maintains a list of any revisions to these restrictions, which may be obtained by writing to that office.

4. Rules. Unless otherwise specified, all normal USCF rules shall govern. For example, both sides are required to keep an accurate score. The only exceptions to normal rules will occur when one or both players are in time trouble (see Rule 9, below).

5. Tournament Director. One or more directors should be available during any sudden-death control, so that any disputes may be settled without delay. All claims, however, whether time forfeits, illegal moves, draws, or others, must be initiated by the players themselves (but see Rule 10.D, below). The tournament director may expel from the room or further penalize any spectator who interferes with a game or calls a player's attention to any available claim. The director is responsible for interpreting all rules.

VARIATION: If it is possible to have a tournament director or deputy watching every game, they may initiate a claim, including a time forfeit, on behalf of a player, but only if this procedure is carried out consistently and announced in advance.

6. Duration of the Game. A player loses on time if he fails to complete all of his moves before his flag falls. It is not necessary that his opponent have a complete and reasonably accurate score sheet.

7. The Won Game.

    A. A game is won by the player:
1. who has mated his opponent's king;
2. whose opponent resigns; or
3. whose opponent's flag falls first, at any time before the game is otherwise ended.

    B. A player must claim a win himself by immediately stopping both clocks and notifying the director. To claim a win under this rule, the player's flag must be up and his opponent's flag must be down after the clocks have been stopped.

8. The Drawn Game. A game is drawn:

    A. if one of the kings is stalemated;

    B. by agreement between the players during a game, not before or after the game;

    C. if both flags are down before a win is claimed;

    D. if a player demonstrates a perpetual check or a forced repetition of position under the conditions of USCF Rule I.12.F;

    E. if neither player has sufficient material for a possible checkmate, as provided in USCF Rule I.12.I;

    F. if one player has insufficient material for a possible checkmate as described in USCF Rule I.12.I, and his opponent's flag falls first.

9. Time Trouble. Time trouble occurs when a player has less than five minutes to complete the game. A player in such a situation:

    A. must handle the clock with the same hand with which he handles his pieces;

B. must remove his hand from the clock button after depressing his button and must keep his hand off the clock until it is time to press it again;

C. must not pick up the clock;

D. must replace pieces on his own time, if he accidentally displaces one or more of them.

If only one player is in time trouble, normal rules apply to the one with more than five minutes left.

10. Miscellaneous.

A. If a player makes an illegal move when time trouble exists and punches his clock, his opponent should immediately stop both clocks and summon the director. After verifying that an illegal move has been made, the tournament director should add two minutes to the time of the opponent. Illegal moves unnoticed by both players when time pressure exists cannot be corrected afterwards.

B. Announcing a check is not required.

C. In case of a dispute, either player may stop the clocks while the director is being summoned.

D. In positions that are clearly drawn, such as positions with no pawns remaining for either side and with greatly simplified material (for example, king and knight versus king and knight), the director may intervene to declare the game a draw. In these same positions either player may stop the clock and ask the director for a draw. If the request is rejected, two minutes will be added to the time of the opponent of the person making the request.

E. Any player using excessive force on a clock may be warned by the director and penalized by up to the loss of the game for a second infraction.

CHAPTER 5

Computer Chess Rules and Regulations

1. Membership

Computer programs may be registered by the originator or the legal owner of the program as Computer Members of the USCF. The dues for Computer Members shall be the same as for regular adult members. The rights and privileges of computer members include and are limited to: the right to play in USCF tournaments, subject to USCF regulations on computer participation; the right to acquire an official USCF rating; and a subscription to *Chess Life* magazine. Specific identification and registration procedures shall be determined administratively.

2. Sale of Membership

Computer memberships may be sold only by the USCF office. Owners are required to sign a statement agreeing to specific rules. Computer memberships are sold only to experimental programs, and owners are required to sign a noncommercial use agreement.

3. Participation in Tournaments

Tournament announcements in *Chess Life* shall specify whether computers may enter by including the symbol "NC" where computers are ineligible. If the director does not so specify, computers may enter, provided such entries are arranged in advance with the director's consent.

4. Pairings

The director shall announce to the participants the presence of one or more computer entrants in a tournament. Within a reasonable time after this announcement, a player has the right to inform the director not to pair him with a computer. A player who does not do so is assumed willing to be paired with a computer. A player who objects to such a pairing shall choose between two categories:

- A. Absolute refusal to play a computer. Such players shall be paired as if they had already played each computer in the tournament.
- B. Preference not to play a computer. Such players may be paired with a computer only in the event that a serious pairing problem would result otherwise, for example if a prize is at stake.

5. Eligibility for Prizes

Computers may win only prizes specifically designated for them. Other prizes shall be distributed as though computers were not entered.

6. Ratings

In a tournament with both human and computer participants, games between computers shall be rated. Directors should avoid pairing two computers when such pairing would result in one computer playing more than half its games against other computers. Tournaments in which only computers participate will be rated at the USCF's discretion, except that matches between two computers will not be rated.

Commercial computers may acquire ratings only through USCF's Computer Rating Agency. Interested manufacturers should write for details. Once a commercial computer has achieved a rating through the USCF Computer Rating Agency, that rating does not vary, even if the computer is entered in other tournaments for testing, promotion, or any other reasons.

7. Consultation

A player who consults a computer for advice about his game shall be subject to the same penalties that he would receive for asking advice from another person.

RULES FOR PLAY INVOLVING COMPUTERS

The following rules are for USCF-rated tournaments when one of the players (or both) is a computer. In matters not covered by these rules, play is governed by applicable human rules, as interpreted by the director. In these rules, the term "computer" refers to a chess program running on a computer. The term "opponent" refers to the computer's opponent, human or computer. The term "operator" refers to the person running the computer. The following rules shall govern play:

1. Parameter Settings

Before play begins, the operator shall do all initial setting up of the computer. At this time, the operator may freely specify any operating parameters, such as rate of play, suggested openings, value of a draw, etc. After play begins, the role of the operator is passive. During the game, the operator is not allowed to alter any parameter settings that might alter the course of the game.

2. Communication of Moves

During play, the operator is to communicate the opponent's moves to the computer.

3. Execution of Moves

The operator is to execute the computer's specified move on the playing chessboard. "Touch" rules do not strictly apply to the operator, but excessive handling of pieces may violate other rules, such as those against distracting the opponent. A piece shall be deemed touched by the computer when a move involving that piece has been communicated by the program to its output device, except that displays of moves it is considering shall not be considered communication of a move. A move for the computer shall be deemed completed when it has been executed on the board by the operator, in accordance with the normal rules.

4. Clock

After the computer's move is executed, the operator is to start the opponent's clock.

5. Reconciliation of Positions

If, during play, different positions should arise on the playing chessboard and the computer's representation thereof, such differences shall be corrected with the assistance of the tournament director. The tournament director may choose either to accept the playing chessboard as official, or to retrace the moves to the point of departure. If the director chooses to back up the game, then he shall readjust the clocks accordingly. The tournament director shall penalize the computer if the score indicates that the computer or its operator has caused the discrepancy of position.

6. Resetting the Computer

If, during play, the computer is unable to accept a legal move because of discrepancies, communication trouble, or computer trouble, then the operator may set up the current board position and status, along with clock times. Other parameters set must be the same as those in effect at the start of the game. The clocks are not stopped during the resetting of the computer nor for any other "down time" (time when the computer is unable to function, despite the efforts of its operator).

7. Clock Times

There shall be a clock at the chessboard whether or not there is an internal clock in the computer. The operator and the opponent shall use the external clock, which shall be the official timer for the game. However, the tournament director may consider the computer's internal clock as evidence in making decisions concerning the game, provided that the opponent approves such use before the information is sought.

The operator may communicate the clock times to the computer only if the computer initiates the request.

8. Memory-Unit Exchange

The operator may change or insert memory units when the computer requests this and identifies the unit to be inserted, by description or by generating a coded signal or message with a single, predetermined meaning. Diskettes, disk cartridges, tapes, ROM cartridges ("program modules" in commercial machines), and the like are all considered equivalent forms of memory units.

9. Draw Offers and Resignation

The operator may offer a draw, accept a draw, or resign on behalf of the computer. This may be done with or without computer consultation.

10. Time Forfeits

The operator may claim the game in cases where the opponent has exceeded the time limit.

11. Adjournments

The operator shall carry out the necessary adjournment formalities.

12. Score

The operator and/or the computer must keep a score of the game.

CHAPTER 6

Rules for Handicapped Players

1. Purpose of the Rules for Handicapped Players

The purpose of these rules for players with temporary or permanent handicaps is to encourage them to play chess. Bearing in mind that there are many kinds of handicaps and many individuals who meet a wide variety of challenges, the tournament director enjoys considerable discretionary authority to institute special rules.

2. Equality of Treatment

Players with handicaps, either temporary or permanent, which prevent them from fulfilling certain conditions of the official rules of chess, shall have special consideration in meeting those rules. Their opponents shall be offered the same consideration. The tournament director is responsible for seeing that both opponents know about and understand any special rules he authorizes. No player may refuse to play a handicapped opponent.

3. Eligibility for USCF Events

To be eligible to compete, a player must be able to communicate his selection of moves in some unambiguous manner that does not require prompting of any kind from any person. An interpreter may be employed.

4. Analogous Situations

When there are doubts concerning what provisions should be made in the rules for handicapped players, the tournament director should consult the following rules for visually handicapped players (closely adapted from FIDE's Rules for the Visually Handicapped) and apply them analogously. These rules apply when one or both players are handicapped.

5. Access

USCF organizers should make every effort to secure sites for their tournaments that are accessible to handicapped players and provided with appropriate facilities for their comfort.

6. The Rules for Visually Handicapped Players (to be applied analogously in the case of other handicaps):

A. A blind player is entitled to use a chessboard with securing apertures, even if a sighted opponent prefers to use a normal board simultaneously. In a game between two blind players, each is entitled to use his own board.

B. The moves shall be announced clearly, repeated by the opponent, and executed on his board.

C. On the blind player's board, a piece shall be deemed "touched" when it has been taken out of the securing aperture.

D. A move shall be deemed completed when—

    a. a piece is placed into a securing aperture;

    b. in the case of a capture, the captured piece has been removed from the board of the player who is on move;

    c. the move has been announced.

    Only after these events shall the opponent's clock be started.

E. A chess clock with a flag made especially for the blind shall be admissible.

F. A blind player may keep the score of the game in braille or on a tape recorder.

G. A slip of the tongue in announcing a move must be corrected immediately and before starting the clock of the opponent.

H. If, during a game, different positions should arise on the two boards, such differences must be corrected with the assistance of the tournament director and with consultation of both players' game scores. In resolving such differences, the player who has recorded the correct move but has made an incorrect one on his board may be penalized by the addition of up to five minutes to his elapsed time.

I. If, when such discrepancies occur, the two game scores are also found to differ, the game shall be reconstructed up to the last point of agreement, and the tournament director shall adjust the clocks accordingly.

J. A blind player shall have the right to make use of an assistant, who shall have any or all of the following duties:

    a. to make the moves of the blind player on the board of the opponent;

    b. to announce the moves of the sighted player;

    c. to keep score for the blind player and to start his opponent's clock;

    d. to inform the blind player, at his request, of the number of moves made and the time consumed by either or both players;

    e. to claim the game in cases when the time limit has been exceeded;

    f. to carry out the necessary formalities in cases when the game is to be adjourned.

If the blind player uses such assistance, the sighted player is entitled to parallel assistance should he so desire.

K. If the blind player does not require any assistance, the sighted player may make use of an assistant who shall announce the sighted player's moves and make the blind player's moves on the sighted player's board.

L. The USCF accepts a state's certification of a person's legal blindness as sufficient evidence of eligibility for tournaments for the blind and for special considerations under these rules, except if that person holds a valid driver's license.

CHAPTER 7

Chess Notation

Since 1981, FIDE has recognized only algebraic notation for its highest-level tournaments and has vigorously encouraged the universal use of this system. USCF officially supports the use of a single, world-wide notation system, but still recognizes other systems, including the older descriptive notation and the newer computer algebraic. These three systems and some variants are described here, along with international correspondence notation.

Algebraic Notation

1. Pieces (except pawns) are identified by an uppercase letter, the first letter of their names. King and knight start with "K", so "N" is used for the knight. Pawn moves are indicated by the absence of such an uppercase letter.

   The names of the pieces vary from language to lan-

guage, of course, so the identifying abbreviations vary
also. Here is a table of the symbols for the pieces in
some major Western languages:

	♚	♛	♜	♝	♞
English	K	Q	R	B	N
German	K	D	T	L	S
Spanish	R	D	T	A	C
French	R	D	T	F	C
Dutch	K	D	T	L	P
Russian	KP	Ф	Л	C	K
Icelandic	K	D	H	B	R
Yugoslav	K	D	T	L	S

2. Squares are identified by a small letter and a number,
   signifying the algebra-like coordinates on the board
   (thus, the name of the system).

   a. The rows of squares going from one player to the
      other ("up and down") are *files*, and are labeled with
      letters *a* through *h*, starting with the row to white's
      left.

   b. The rows of squares going from the left to the right
      edge of the board are *ranks* and are labeled with
      numbers 1 through 8, starting at white's side of the

board. At the start of the game, therefore, white's more major pieces are on the first rank and pawns on the second; black's are on the eighth and seventh respectively.

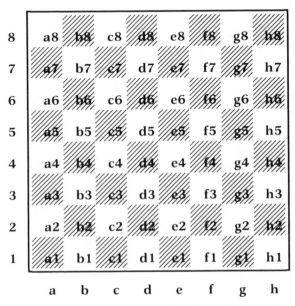

3. Moves are indicated by combining the symbol for the piece and its arrival square, for example, Be5, Rh6, Nf6. Pawn moves indicate only the arrival square, for example, e4, c5, g3.

4. Captures are indicated by inserting an *x* (pronounced "takes") between the piece symbol and the arrival square, for example, Bxe5, Rxh6, Nxf6.

Because there is no abbreviation used for pawns, pawn captures include the original file, the x, and the arrival square, for example, cxd4, exf5, gxh7. In the case of a capture *en passant*, the arrival square is the one on which the capturing pawn finally rests, and "e.p." is added to the notation, for example, 14. f4, gxf3 e.p.

5. In cases where these brief notations would be ambiguous, clarification is achieved first by adding the original file of the moving piece or second by adding the rank of the moving piece:

   a. If both rooks are on the first rank and one of them moves to d1, the notation might be Rad1.

   b. If both knights are on the f file and one moves to e5, adding the original file would be useless, so the move is either N3e5 or N7e5.

   c. If knights are at f3 and c2 and one of them moves to d4, the file is the clarifier: Nfd4 or Ncd4. If this move is a capture, the x goes between the piece identifier (Nf or Ne) and the arrival square: Nfxd4.

6. Special symbols:

O-O	castling kingside
O-O-O	castling queenside
X	captures or takes (an earlier version of algebraic notation used a colon instead)
+	check (sometimes "ch.")
++	checkmate
=	a pawn promotion, as in f8=Q or d1=N.
e.p.	*en passant*

Figurine Algebraic

   This system is exactly like regular algebraic, except the abbreviations of the pieces are replaced by internationally recognized symbols: ♚ ♛ ♜ ♝ ♞ . This system is obviously advantageous for publications but not practical for players in the tournament hall.

Long Algebraic

This system is just like normal algebraic, except that it prevents the possibility of ambiguities by indicating departure as well as arrival square for each move. A sample game might start 1 c2-c4 Ng8-f6, 2 Nbl-c3 g7-g6, 3 d2-d4 Bf8-g7, and so forth.

Computer Notation

This variation of long algebraic eliminates the abbreviation of the pieces as redundant. Written versions usually use capital letters rather than the small ones otherwise associated with squares.

The sample moves shown in the long algebraic paragraph would be written 1 C2-C4 G8-F6, 2 Bl-C3 G7-G6, 3 D2-D4 F8-G7. Captures are written with hyphens also (instead of x's).

One difference between this system and others is in the notation for castling. Computer notation indicates simply the departure and arrival square of the king: E1-G1, E1-C1, E8-G8, or E8-C8.

This code is necessary for playing chess with microcomputers without sensory boards and with personal computers and other machines that receive communications through a keyboard.

English Descriptive Notation

1. Pieces (including pawns) are identified by their initials, as in algebraic. Those that begin the game on the side of the board nearer the king sometimes have a K in front of their own initial; those on the queen's side of the board a Q.

2. The files are named for the pieces originally occupying them: QR, QN, QB, Q, K, KB, KN, KR.

3. The ranks are numbered from each player's point of view, from 1 to 8. White's pieces and pawns begin the game on the first and second ranks from white's point of view, the eighth and seventh respectively from black's point of view.

4. Each square has two names, one from each player's point of view. The white QR, for example, starts the game at white's QR1 and black's QR8. White's K4 is black's K5, and so forth.

5. Each pawn is named by the file on which it stands: QRP, QNP, QBP, QP, KP, KBP, KNP, and KRP.

6. A move to a vacant square is indicated by the name of piece, a hyphen, and the name of the arrival square. Although clarity is necessary, every attempt is made to eliminate redundancy. For example, P-K4 is a standard notation, as KP-K4 repeats the registry of movement on the K-file. N-KB3 is preferred to KN-B3 unless the QN could also reach the B3 square, for example, from Q2.

7. A capture is indicated by the abbreviation of the capturing piece, an *x*, and the abbreviation of the captured piece, for example, BxN, or QRxP (necessary if the KR also attacked a pawn), or PxKP (necessary if a pawn attacked more than one pawn), and so forth.

8. If the K and Q prefixes do not clarify a potential ambiguity, or if the pieces have made enough moves so that the original designations are no longer clear or particularly relevant, clarity is achieved with a slash

and a rank number after the piece symbol. For example, if either of two knights could capture a bishop, the notation might be N/4xB.

9. A check ("ch") is sometimes enough to clarify an ambiguity, for example, B-N5 ch, even if both bishops could reach N5 squares.

10. Castling kingside is indicated by O-O; queenside by O-O-O.

11. A pawn promotion is indicated by the move, a slash, and the symbol for the new piece. Examples: P-B8/Q, or PxR/N.

Sample Game

Here, without further comment, is a sample game fragment written in each of the three common notations:

Algebraic		*Computer*		*Descriptive*	
1. e4	e5	E2-E4	E7-E5	P-K4	P-K4
2. Nf3	Nc6	G1-F3	B8-C6	N-KB3	N-QB3
3. Bb5	a6	F1-B5	A7-A6	B-N5	P-QR3
4. Bxc6	dxc6	B5-C6	D7-C6	BxN	QPxB
5. d3	Bb4+	D2-D3	F8-B4	P-Q3	B-N5ch
6. Nc3	Nf6	B1-C3	G8-F6	N-B3	N-B3
7. O-O	Bxc3	E1-G1	B4-C3	O-O	BxN

If you have played through the notation of your choice accurately, you should have reached the following position on your board:

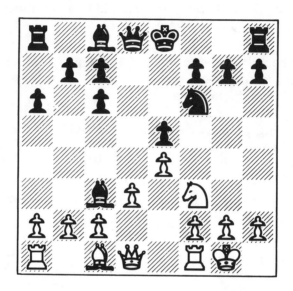

International Correspondence Notation

To avoid language problems—including different alphabets—international correspondence players use an all-numeric system that is otherwise very similar to computer notation.

1. Each square is designated by a two-digit number, as indicated below. The first digit is a replacement of 1–8 for the a–h files, the second is the conventional rank number.

Black

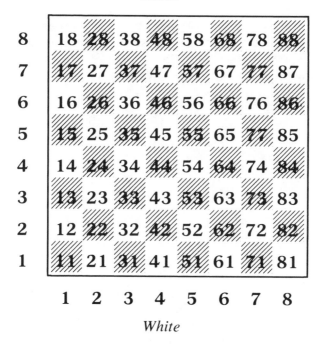

	1	2	3	4	5	6	7	8
8	18	28	38	48	58	68	78	88
7	17	27	37	47	57	67	77	87
6	16	26	36	46	56	66	76	86
5	15	25	35	45	55	65	77	85
4	14	24	34	44	54	64	74	84
3	13	23	33	43	53	63	73	83
2	12	22	32	42	52	62	72	82
1	11	21	31	41	51	61	71	81

White

2. A move is indicated by a four-digit number that combines the departure and arrival squares without punctuation. For example, 5254 is the same as e4 or P-K4.

3. Castling is noted as a king move: 5171, 5131, 5878, or 5838.

4. For pawn promotions, the first two digits indicate the departure square, the third the arrival file, and the fourth the new piece (1=Q, 2=R, 3=B, 4=N).

Telephone and Radio Notation

When players or their agents relay moves with their voices, some confusion can arise because b, c, d, e, and g can all sound rather alike. The potential difficulty is solved by using algebraic notation with a variation of the military alphabet, e.g., able, baker, charlie, david, easy, fox, george, harry.

CHAPTER 8

Equipment Standards

The three elements of chess equipment, pieces, boards, and clocks, are each discussed in detail below. In general, simple, functional designs are preferred for use in official competitions so players, directors, and spectators are not distracted by ornateness, unusual design, or other aesthetic values. Designer and decorator pieces are available, which serve good purposes other than as suitable equipment for tournament chess.

If the organizer of the tournament provides equipment conforming to the standards set forth below, then the players should use that equipment. If the organizer does not provide one or more elements of the equipment, the players should agree on any that meets the standards or, failing such agreement, play with black's choice, if it meets the standards. If black does not provide standard equipment and white does, black does not have the right to delay the start of the game to search for alternative equipment. The chief tournament director is the final arbiter of whether the equipment in question conforms to standards. (But see note, p. 132, regarding a late player.)

Chess Pieces

Material

Pieces should be made of wood, plastic, or similarly smooth, dense materials.

Size

The king's height should be 3⅜–4⅛ inches (8.5–10.5 cm). The diameter of the king's base should be 40%–50% of the height. The other pieces should be proportionate in height and form. Pieces with extra weights in their bases are preferable, but all should be well balanced for stability and comfortable moving.

Form

The conventional "Staunton" pattern is the standard, though minor variations in design are of little consequence, so long as the pieces are clearly distinguishable from each other and generally conform to this pattern. In particular, the king and queen should have clearly different tops. The bishop's top may have an angled groove or a knob of a different color to distinguish it from a pawn.

Color

Pieces should be the colors of naturally light and dark wood (for example, maple or boxwood and walnut or ebony) or approximations of these colors, such as simply white and black. Most players prefer a matte (nonshiny) finish.

Chessboards

Material

Any smooth material that allows the easy movement of pieces is acceptable. Satisfactory boards have been made of wood, plastic, paper, cardboard, cloth, and stone, especially marble.

Color

Like the pieces, chessboard colors should offer high contrast between the light and dark sections yet remain pleasing to the eye. Walnut or teak against maple or birch makes an ideal combination. Other combinations include green or brown against ivory or buff. The colors and the finish should allow extended examination without eyestrain. Squares that do not exactly match the colors of the pieces (for example, green and buff) are popular because they allow ready distinction between empty and occupied squares. The conventional red and black checkerboard is almost universally eschewed by chess players.

Proportions

The pieces should fit comfortably on the board, being neither too crowded nor too isolated on the squares. The king and queen, for example, should fit on a square so that they do not touch any edge. Squares of approximately 2–2½ inches (5–6.5 cm) are about right for standard sets. One convenient test is that the square formed by the bases of four pawns should be slightly larger than any square on their board.

Borders

The width of the border around the squares is a matter of personal taste, so long as it does not affect a player's conveniently reaching the pieces. Some borders include aids to scorekeeping in the form of letters and numbers for the algebraic system of notation, and some do not. Both designs are acceptable.

Tables

A table with an inset or otherwise fitted chessboard is very satisfactory. The playing surface should be about 30 inches from the ground (normal table height). If the board is not fastened to the table, it should remain stationary. Any table used in competition should provide ample room for the clock, captured pieces, score sheets, players' elbows or forearms, and light refreshments around the actual chessboard.

Clocks

Chess clocks should be as accurate and as silent as possible. They should have a device that clearly signals the end of a time control, such as a "flag" that falls when the minute hand reaches the mark at the figure 12. The flag should be of a size and color so as to be clearly visible to players and directors.

The digital clocks introduced in recent years are not yet fully acceptable as tournament equipment in all circumstances. In the abstract, they fully meet the essential demands of accuracy, silence, and a signaling device (they beep or cease operating instead of having a flag). Some players have difficulty with the digital readout. Others object to a sound signal (a beep instead of a mechanical click) when one clock stops and the other starts. Others have difficulty seeing from a distance which player is due to move.

Until such objections are overcome by time and familiarity, owners and advocates of these devices should not expect to force their use on opponents. If digital clocks are used in competition, the providers should explain all relevant operational facts (for example, the signal at the end of a control, a display change from minutes to seconds, the resetting procedure, and so forth) to both the opponent and the director. A conventional, analog clock is more "standard" than a digital clock and may be used even if black supplies and prefers the digital model.

NOTE: If black is late for the start of a round, the choice of equipment falls to white. Black may not object unless white's choice is for nonstandard equipment, in which case black's clock continues to run while substitutions are made. The discretion of the director will decide questionable cases.

CHAPTER 9

Players' Rights and Responsibilities

Every Player Has the Right to Expect:

1. That the tournament director is reliable and has a knowledge of the laws of chess, as per USCF standards.

2. That the tournament director has in his possession an official USCF rulebook on the premises during the tournament.

3. That any special rules that are pertinent to that particular tournament will be announced and posted, for example, 50-move rules, tie-break system, time-forfeit procedure, and so forth.

4. That the pairing system used is fair and impartial and that it will be administered uniformly.

5. That the starting time of the rounds will be posted and that the rounds will start reasonably on time.

6. That conditions such as lighting, space requirements, noise, etc., be at an acceptable level conducive to good competition.

7. That tournament directors be available in case of protests and at all time controls.

8. That the round results will be posted in a timely fashion.

9. That upon request, a tournament director will initiate the appeals process and appoint an Appeals Committee.

Players' Responsibilities

1. To conduct themselves in an orderly fashion.

2. To compete in a spirit of good sportsmanship.

3. To be present at the starting time for each round.

4. To obey the laws of chess.

5. To conform to the USCF code of ethics.

CHAPTER 10

USCF Code of Ethics

PURPOSE

1. The purpose of the rules and procedures set forth in this code of ethics is to provide articulated ethical standards to which the conduct of players, tournament directors, sponsors, and other individuals and entities participating in or otherwise connected with tournaments, events, or other activities sponsored by the USCF and/or its affiliates is to be conformed; to provide specified sanctions for conduct that does not conform to such standards; and to provide the procedures by which alleged violations are to be investigated and, if necessary, the appropriate sanctions to be imposed.

2. The standards, sanctions, and procedures set forth in the code of ethics are not equivalent to criminal laws and procedure inasmuch as they do not concern personal liberty or property rights. Rather, the code of

ethics is concerned with the rights and privileges of membership in the USCF, including, but not limited to, the privilege of participating in tournaments, events, or other activities as a member of the USCF.

3. The standards, sanctions, and procedures set forth in this code of ethics shall apply only to (A) actions and behavior that occur in connection with tournaments, events, or other activities sponsored by the USCF or its affiliates; or (B) individuals or entities who misrepresent the nature or extent of their association with the USCF or its affiliates.

4. By applying for such membership, each member of the USCF agrees to be bound by this code of ethics.

STANDARD OF CONDUCT

5. The actions and behavior of players, tournament directors, sponsors, and other individuals and entities participating in or otherwise connected with tournaments, events, or other activities sponsored by the USCF and/ or its affiliates shall, in general, be in accordance with the spirit of fair play and good sportsmanship, which the USCF and its affiliates, sponsors, and members have a right to expect from such participants, as illustrated by the examples below.

6. The following list does not purport to be a complete itemization of all actions and behavior that are considered unethical:

   A. Repeated or gross violation of chess proprieties or tournament regulations;

B. Accusations of unethical conduct at a USCF-sanctioned event, unless made in private to a tournament director or other official;

C. Playing in a USCF game or tournament when under suspension;

D. Betting on the results of any USCF-sponsored game or tournament;

E. Repeated or gross antisocial behavior at the site of a USCF-sponsored game or tournament;

F. Nonpayment of any justified sums owed the USCF or any of its affiliates;

G. Influencing or attempting to influence an entrant to withdraw from any event sponsored by the USCF or any of its affiliates; or

H. Actions that bring disrepute on the game of chess.

PROCEDURES

7. Any member, sponsor, affiliate, or official of the USCF may initiate procedures under this code of ethics. In the case of each alleged violation, the following steps shall occur:

A. A factual inquiry shall be made by the Ethics Committee, assisted as necessary by the USCF staff;

B. Appropriate sanctions, if any, shall be imposed by the Committee;

   C. Such sanctions shall be deemed final, unless appealed to the Policy Board by the person or persons against whom sanctions have been imposed or upon the initiative of a member of the Policy Board;

   D. Upon appeal, a review of the facts and the appropriateness of the sanctions shall be undertaken by the full Board; and

   E. The sanctions shall be either continued, modified, or revoked.

8. In the case of any factual inquiry pursuant to step A and, if appropriate, step D above, the member challenged shall: receive notice of the date, time, and place of hearing; be furnished in writing with a description of the alleged violation; have the right to produce evidence on his behalf and to be present when any evidence is produced against him; and have the right to be present during the entire hearing.

SANCTIONS

9. In the case of every sanction that results in suspension or expulsion, a member may not participate in any USCF-sponsored tournament, event, or activity, including but not limited to:

   A. Acting as nonplaying captain,

   B. Kibitzing any game or event,

   C. Being physically present at the site of a tournament, or

D. Participating in the corporate or business affairs of USCF or any affiliated organization.

10. Paragraphs 11 through 16 set forth suggested sanctions that may be imposed by appropriate disciplinary bodies. The disciplinary body imposing the sanction may choose to issue a lesser or greater sanction than those set forth herein; likewise, it may vary, combine, or impose sanctions not set forth below.

REPRIMAND

11. A determination that a member has committed an offense warranting discipline becomes a matter of record, but no further sanction is imposed at the time. A reprimand automatically carries a probation of at least three months; if the member is adjudged guilty of another offense during that period, he is then liable to further sanctions for both offenses.

CENSURE

12. A determination that a member has committed a serious offense warranting discipline becomes a matter of record, but no further sanction is imposed at the time. Censure carries a probationary period of at least one year; if the member is adjudged guilty of another offense during that period, he is liable to further sanction for both offenses.

SUSPENDED SENTENCE WITH PROBATION

13. A determination is made that a member has committed an offense warranting discipline. When the discipline is

imposed and execution thereof suspended, such suspension shall include probation for at least six months longer than the discipline imposed. If a member is adjudged guilty of another offense during the period of probation, unless otherwise decreed, the original discipline shall be added to such discipline as may be imposed for the new offense.

SUSPENSION

14. Suspension is a determination that a member has committed an offense warranting abrogation, for a specified period of time, of all membership rights and privileges.

EXPULSION

15. Expulsion is a determination that a member has committed an offense warranting the permanent abrogation of all membership rights and privileges, including but not limited to those set forth in Paragraph 9 above. An expelled member may be readmitted to membership only by the USCF Policy Board. No application for reinstatement may be considered before two years from the date of expulsion.

EXCLUSION FROM EVENTS

16. This is a more selective determination that a member has committed an offense warranting abrogation of a member's right to play in certain specified events.

17. The effective date of a sanction imposed on a judged member shall be that date named by the Committee in its determination or, failing that, five days after oral or written notification of such sanction to the judged member.

18. The USCF business office shall be advised of each such notice, either orally or in writing, and such notice shall declare the date upon which the sanction became effective. The business office shall in turn report each such sanction to the members of the Policy Board.

CHAPTER 11

Chess Ratings

Tournament results, pairing rules, and ratings are so inter-dependent that each player should have at least a good idea of how chess ratings operate. The details of the system are complicated, but they are free for the asking from USCF.

Every player in a sanctioned tournament gets a rating. This rating goes up or down with nearly every game played because it is a measure of the player's results against his particular opposition.

Example 1: A previously unrated player plays six games against opponents whose ratings average 1500. He wins three and loses three. He starts with a "provisional" rating of 1500, the average of his opponents because he had an "average" score against them. His first rating would be the same if he had drawn all six games or had any other combination of results that led to a 3–3 score.

The rating system is built on the theory that equally

rated players will have equal results, each winning two games out of four. A player with a 200-point advantage on his opponent will win about three times out of four. The odds lengthen to almost certainty when the rating advantage is about 400 points.

This theory gives us the starting point for first ratings. We know that a player won or lost a game (or drew), so his first result is his opponent's rating plus or minus 400 points if he won or lost (if he drew, it is his opponent's rating). This theory is applied to the first 20 games of a player, the life of his "provisional" rating.

Example 2: A previously unrated player beats a 1212, loses to an 1815, beats a 1340, and draws a 1438. The calculation is easy:

$$1212 + 400 = 1612$$
$$1815 - 400 = 1415$$
$$1340 + 400 = 1740$$
$$1438 \qquad = 1438$$

$$\frac{1551.25}{4)6205}$$

His first rating will be 1551.

This rating, left unchanged, will be published as 1551/4, indicating that it is based on only four games. The fewer games played, the less reliable the rating.

Example 3: This player, with a 1551/4 rating, enters another tournament. He beats a 1472, loses to a 1726 and a 1637, and draws a 1595. The same thinking applies, but his old rating times the number of games it represents must be added so the average will be properly weighted:

$$4 \times 1551 \quad = 6204$$
$$1472 + 400 = 1872$$
$$1726 - 400 = 1326$$
$$1637 - 400 = 1237$$
$$1595 \qquad = 1595$$

$$\begin{array}{r} 1529.25 \\ \hline 8)\overline{12234} \end{array}$$

His rating drops to 1529/8.

These calculations can be done algebraically with the following formula:

$$R_p = R_c + \frac{400\ (W - L)}{N}$$

where R_p is the new rating, R_c the average rating of opponents, W the number of wins, L the number of losses, and N the number of games.

The formula and procedure for players with "established" ratings, based on more than 20 games, is somewhat different and much more complicated, but the principles remain similar. The current system is a refinement of the older one that viewed each game as a kind of wager for rating points.

If equally rated players draw, there is no change. If one wins, he goes up 16 points and the loser goes down 16. Additionally, there is a "handicap" of up to 16 points for rating differences, increasing or decreasing the 16-point exchange as appropriate.

For example, if the favored player outrates his opponent by 200 points, he is supposed to win three out of four. If he wins a single game, he gets only half the 16 he would get against an equal opponent. The opponent loses 8. If the underdog wins, he gets 24 points, and the favorite loses that many.

If these players contest a four-game match and the favorite wins by a 3–1 score, his rating change is + 8 + 8 + 8 − 24 = 0. In the long run, a player's rating does not change if he performs exactly as the system predicts he will. The more varied his results, the more his rating will fluctuate.

The rating procedure for established players also includes bonus points for those who do exceptionally well in an event. Since such players were better than their pretournament ratings predicted them to be, players who get bonuses generate "feedback" points to their opponents.

The average USCF rating is about 1500, about 1550 for active tournament players. For purposes of general identification and often for the awarding of tournament prizes, rated players are grouped as follows:

Name	Rating Range	Percentile
Senior Master	above 2399	99
Master	2200–2399	97–98
Expert	2000–2199	89–96
Class A	1800–1999	77–88
Class B	1600–1799	59–76
Class C	1400–1599	41–58
Class D	1200–1399	22–40
Class E	below 1200	1–21

International (FIDE) ratings are calculated somewhat differently. They are published for men rated over 2200 and women rated over 1900.

FIDE Masters earn their titles by ratings, but the higher

titles of International Master and International Grandmaster require outstanding performances in a number of high-level events. These titles, unlike ratings and most USCF titles, are lifetime awards.

CHAPTER 12

Correspondence Chess

Correspondence chess, though often identified with its most popular form, postal chess, actually embraces all the forms of chess competition that do not involve a face-to-face, over-the-board contest between the contestants. Its roots are allegedly medieval, as noblemen are said to have dispatched messengers with moves to rivals who lived at considerable distance—all without benefit of convenient and standardized notation. Today, correspondence chess includes communication by postal means, by telephone, radio, telex and telegraph, and, of course, by computer. There has even been a simultaneous exhibition match by satellite TV.

The rules for these contests vary, and they are not even fully standardized within each form of correspondence. In general, they attempt to approximate tournament chess as closely as possible, while still taking advantage of the opportunities provided by the communication system, and the generally more leisurely pace provided for the games.

In team telephone and telex matches, variations from the rules and normal time controls are minimal. Players are held strictly to the normal rules by an onsite director, and moves are communicated to the opponent by messengers and runners. One of the few differences between these competitions and games in a tournament hall is that neither player is charged with the time used in this communication. Each player, therefore, gains some extra reflection time, which is usually somewhat balanced by a faster-than-normal time control.

In postal chess, however, and in other forms designed to take more than an afternoon or evening to complete, the rules have to be substantially different. There is no way, for example, to enforce rules against researching openings and endings or against manipulating pieces before deciding on a move. These practices are, therefore, virtually encouraged in the interest of more accurate, perfect chess, unhindered by the relentless ticking of the chess clock or the other pressures of the tournament hall.

Nevertheless, each player is expected to rely on his own resources, his memory and talent and library. Consulting another person is strictly unethical and a proven violation is usually cause for forfeiture. Similarly, using a chess computer or program for analysis is unethical at this time, and this practice may carry severe penalties.

Time limits, of course, have to be different from over-the-board (OTB) chess. Typically, neither player is charged for the time moves spend in the control of the postal service. Some organizations require that a player respond to a move within 2–4 days of receiving it. Even more commonly, players are given a time budget to use at their discretion, for example, 30 days in which to make 10 moves. Most contests allow limited time-outs for vacations, illness, or other emergencies.

A special difficulty in correspondence chess is in illegal, illegible, or ambiguous moves. It is a nuisance to receive such a move, as clarification can take a week or more of transit time, during which the game is stalled. Such moves are sometimes caused by an inaccurate position on a player's board, for example, after someone has played through some combinational variations without resetting the game position accurately.

In such situations, whatever their cause, USCF postal rules call for an application of a "touch-move" analogy. If a piece has been moved to an impossible square, for example, the player must move the same piece to a possible square. Or if an illegal capture has been made, the player must capture the same piece legally, if possible. As in OTB chess, if no legal move is available for a "touched" piece, the player may substitute any legal move. The tournament director, however, may impose a time penalty for the delay caused by such a faulty transmission.

Each organization that sponsors postal chess tournaments, including USCF, publishes detailed rules explaining its own handling of these and other circumstances that differ from OTB situations.

CHAPTER 13

Tournament Directors' Checklists

The following checklists are guides. They may be expanded or contracted, but they are a good starting point for everyone.

PACKING LIST

The following items should be neatly and conveniently arranged in your tournament briefcase or suitcase:

A. General Chess Stationery

—blank pairing cards (one color per section)
—blank wall charts (one color per section)
—blank pairing sheets (one color per section)
—score sheets (lots)
—sealed-move envelopes

—membership forms
  —USCF
  —state association
  —local club
—tournament report form
—financial-report guideline form
—tournament registration forms (a special one for this
  event?)
—handful of "USCF Rating System" handout

B. Other Chess Supplies and Equipment

—latest edition *Official Rules of Chess*
—Tournament Director (TD) ID card
—TD cap, vest, armband, or other identifying clothing
—box for receiving score sheets or results slips (with clear
  sign)
—tie-break sign
—tournament procedures sign and/or handouts
—time-control signs
—round-time signs
—sign and/or handouts about rules and pairing variations
—sign and/or handouts about sudden-death rules
—at least one clock for emergencies
—boards and sets
—board numbers
—rating lists
  —annuals as far back as possible
  —the latest cumulative supplement
  —any supplement(s) since the cumulative
—spare copies of *Chess Life* for new players

C. General Stationery Supplies

—lined note pad
—unlined paper and posterboard for signs

—memo pad
—carbon paper
—receipt book
—thumbtacks
—masking tape
—cellophane tape in dispenser
—paper clips, large and small
—stapler and extra staples
—duct tape
—rubber bands
—ballpoint pens in different colors
—felt-tipped pens—fine, medium, broad—in colors
—pens or pencils to lend players
—ruler
—large eraser
—liquid paper
—adhesive labels
—pencil sharpener
—business envelopes
—return-address stickers
—stamps
—checkbook
—calculator with strong batteries
—business cards
—Band-Aids
—aspirin

D. Special for This Tournament

—advance publicity
—*Chess Life* issue(s)
—fliers or mail-outs
—completed pairing cards of advance entries
—checks and cash from advance entries
—correspondence from advance entries
—currency/change for registration

—trophies
—special prizes
—list of things yet to do for this event
—fliers for coming events

PLANNING AND ACTION CHECKLIST

A. Before Registration

—review *Official Rules of Chess*
—meet with organizers and site/hotel staff
    —tie-break system
    —prizes
    —learn site facilities
    —copy machine and access to it
    —keys to playing room, TD office, skittles area
    —trash cans
    —water supplies
    —check (improve) table layout
    —rope off top boards?
    —learn light switches
    —test for burnt-out bulbs
    —test microphone system
    —determine key locations (TD table, score-sheet distribution and receiving, wall chart and pairing posting, and so forth)
    —determine any restrictions on posting
    —prepare for computers and wheelchairs
    —tape down cords/wires/door bolts with duct tape
—acquire and review advance entries
    —names
    —USCF ID numbers
    —expiration dates
    —ratings
    —half-point byes

—planned round forfeits
—meet with TD staff (see separate list)
—organize for registration

B. During Registration

—double-check everything, especially ratings that look like
  dates (for example 1287, 1185)
—make sure cash control is working
—review the work of all assistants
—make final decision about acceleration of pairings

C. After First Round Begins

—put out box for score sheets or results slips
—lock doors not needed for access
—distribute keys as needed
—post announcements and signs
    —prizes, including specials
    —tie breaks
    —rules and pairing variations
    —time controls
    —time of rounds
    —hotel checkout times
    —sign-up sheets (hotel guests, eligibility for special
      prizes, etc.)
—message box/system for TD staff
—learn nearby restaurants
—arrange for management of equipment
—will tablecloths be changed?
—number pairing cards
—complete and post wall charts ASAP
—check out registration exceptions
    —memberships
    —ID numbers
    —ratings

—names
—addresses
—financial questions

D. After Last Round Begins

—complete room night list for hotel (or remind organizer)
—get USCF conditional credit slip from organizer
—assist in preparation of financial report
—prepare prize-list worksheet, filling in as possible

E. After Tournament Is Over

—complete prize-list worksheet
—collect everything posted on walls
—get money for ratings (including cross-table)
—get money for expenses and fee
—mail report form and wall-chart copies ASAP
—remind organizer to submit memberships instantly
—remind organizer to report results to media instantly
—get names and addresses to local clubs
—get other information to whomever you promised it
—get some sleep

ANNOUNCEMENT CHECKLIST

—organizer's welcome and other remarks
—introduce TD staff
—thanks to others who deserve it
—introduce titled players/other VIPs
—result reporting system
—hands off wall charts
—score-sheet submission (including brilliancy notes)
—round times
—time controls

—special rules and variations
—smoking rules
—silence in tournament hall
—hotel checkout rules
—locations
    —skittles
    —rest rooms
    —food
    —book and equipment sales

NOTE: Keep it short, sweet, and essential. Save announcements of coming events until before a later round—the players are eager to start the first round.

STAFF-MEETING CHECKLIST

—determine experience of everyone unknown
—delegate setup tasks
    —board numbering
    —sets and boards
    —table rearranging
    —score-sheet/handout distribution
—review locations, general site, and tournament hall
—review supplies
—assign tasks (experience/competence, variety, balance)
    —registration
    —tournament
—assign schedules, including break rules
—registration plan
    —money
    —USCF credentials
    —state membership
    —rating
—message-box system
—hotel-room extensions or other phone numbers

—review special tournament rules
  —adjournments
  —computers
  —handicapped
  —appeals
  —pairings
  —byes
  —other
—TD rules and procedures
  —visibility
  —courtesy
  —covering for meal and other breaks
  —circle unplayed games everywhere
  —pencil, pen, or felt-tip and what color(s)?
  —no playing chess, cards, or backgammon!
  —slow, careful posting on everything
  —information on pairing sheets
  —withdrawal procedures (red-X the pairing card and
    note on wall chart)
  —uniform procedures, pairing chart to cards to wall
    charts to point group stacks (highest group on left,
    lowest pairing number on top)
—round times
—time controls
—time-forfeit procedures
—any questions on rules or other topics?

CHAPTER 14

FIDE-Rated Tournaments

All Tournaments

A. At least four FIDE-rated players. (Ratings are published every January 1 and July 1. A rating is not official until it has been published. When a player has been inactive for three years, his rating is dropped from the list but remains official.)

B. A time limit no faster than 23/1 at any stage of the game—40/2½, 45/2½, 40/2, and 30/1½ are common.

C. No more than two rounds a day.

D. At least five rounds.

E. A duration of not more than three months.

F. Prior registration with FIDE through the national federation, preferably two months before the event.

Futurity Round Robins

A. At least 10 players. Smaller tournaments can be rated, but nine games are needed for a publishable rating.

B. At least ⅓ of the players must be FIDE rated. (Women rated 2200 or less may be counted toward this minimum, but doing so would lessen the chance of generating new ratings.) At least one extra rated player is recommended.

C. A reasonable field of non-FIDE-rated players. Ideally, all players should be capable of scoring 40% or more against the rated players. Admitting players with USCF ratings below 2100 is not recommended.

D. A reasonable prize fund to attract the rated players is important. Typically, rated players play free, with entry fees from the others (and donations?) generating the cash.

International Round Robin

A. At least three national federations, including the host federation, must be represented.

B. No more than 20% of the players can be unrated.

C. At least half the players must be titled (GM, IM, or FM) or FIDE rated over 2300.

D. There must be at least nine rounds.

E. For purposes of achieving IM and GM norms, tournaments are assigned categories based on average rating (unrateds count as 2200 for this purpose, but not for rating purposes). The following table shows what scores are necessary in tournaments of various categories and various numbers of rounds, and how many IMs/GMs must be included.

Swisses

A. Players' results are rated individually. All games between rated players will be rated, but an unrated player must play at least four rated players in order to secure a ratable performance. (A good rough measure is performance rating: add 400 points to the ratings of those you beat, subtract 400 from those who beat you, take the rating of those with whom you draw, and average it out. If the result is 2202.5 or better, you have a ratable performance.)

B. Swiss results are valid for title norms if the requirements listed in the international round-robin section are met. One's own rating is averaged in to determine the "field."

C. At least 1/2 of the players must be FIDE rated.

CHART OF POINTS REQUIRED FOR

Nr. of part.	games	required players not from one and the same feder.	minimum rated players	number of titleholders all inclusive		FIDE TITLE RESULT	I 2251 2275	II 2276 2300	III 2301 2325
10	9	4	8	5	3 GM	GM	7	7	6½
					2 GM/3 IM	IM			
11	10	4	9	6	3 GM	GM	8	7½	7
					2 GM/3 IM	IM			
12	11	4	10	6	3 GM	GM	8½	8	8
					2 GM/3 IM	IM			
13	12	5	11	7	3 GM	GM	9½	9	8½
					2 GM/3 IM	IM			
14	13	5	12	7	3 GM	GM	10	9½	9½
					2 GM/3 IM	IM			
15	14	5	12	8	3 GM	GM	11	10½	10
					2 GM/3 IM	IM			
16	15	6	13	8	3 GM	GM	11½	11	10½
					2 GM/3 IM	IM			
17	16	6	14	9	3 GM	GM	12½	12	11½
					2 GM/3 IM	IM			
18	17	6	15	9	3 GM	GM	13	12½	12
					2 GM/3 IM	IM			
19	18	7	16	10	3 GM	GM	14	13½	13
					2 GM/3 IM	IM			
20	19	7	16	10	3 GM	GM	14½	14	13½
					2 GM/3 IM	IM			

FIDE INTERNATIONAL TITLE RESULTS

CATEGORIES AND AVERAGE RATINGS

IV	V	VI	VII	VIII	IX	X	XI	XII	XIII	XIV	XV	XVI
2326	2351	2376	2401	2426	2451	2476	2501	2526	2551	2576	2601	2626
2350	2375	2400	2425	2450	2475	2500	2525	2550	2575	2600	2625	2650
			7	7	6½	6	6	5½	5½	5	4½	4½
6	6	5½	5½	5	4½	4½	4	4	3½	3	3	
			8	7½	7	7	6½	6	6	5½	5	5
7	6½	6	6	5½	5	5	4½	4	4	3½	3	
			8½	8	8	7½	7	7	6½	6	5½	5½
7½	7	7	6½	6	5½	5½	5	4½	4	4	3½	
			9½	9	8½	8	8	7½	7	6½	6	6
8	8	7½	7	6½	6	6	5½	5	4½	4	4	
			10	9½	9½	9	8½	8	7½	7	6½	6½
9	8½	8	7½	7	6½	6½	6	5½	5	4½	4	
			11	10½	10	9½	9	8½	8	7½	7	7
9½	9	8½	8	7½	7	7	6	6	5	5	4½	
			11½	11	10½	10	10	9	8½	8	7½	7
10	10	9	8½	8	7½	7	6½	6	5½	5	4½	
			12½	12	11½	11	10½	10	9½	8½	8	7½
11	10½	10	9½	8½	8	7½	7	6½	6	5½	5	
			13	12½	12	11½	11	10½	10	9	8½	8
11½	11	10½	10	9	8½	8	7½	7	6½	6	5½	
			14	13½	13	12½	11½	11	10½	9½	9	8½
12½	11½	11	10½	9½	9	8½	8	7½	6½	6	5½	
			14½	14	13½	13	12½	11½	11	10½	9½	9
13	12½	11½	11	10½	9½	9	8½	8	7	6½	6	

The average rating consists of a rating figure (from 3.2, 3.4 or 4.4) for each player, which have been totalled and then divided by the number of players. Roundings of the average ratings are made to the nearest whole number. The fraction 0.5 is rounded off upward.

CHAPTER 15

FIDE Regulations for Five-Minute Chess

Approved by the 1977 Central Committee Meeting

To be applied in FIDE tournaments and strongly recommended to be used in all other international five-minute lightning tournaments.

Duration of the Game

1. Each player must make all his moves within five minutes on his clock.

The Clock

2. All the clocks must have a special device, usually a "flag," marking the end of the time-control period.

3. Before play begins, the players should inspect the position of the pieces and the setting of the clock. If they have omitted to do this, no claim shall be accepted after each player has made his first move.

4. Each player must handle the clock with the same hand with which he handles his pieces. *Exception:* It is permitted to perform the castling move by using both hands.

5. The arbiter should stipulate at the beginning of the tournament the direction the clocks are to face, and the player with the black pieces decides on which side of the board he will sit.

6. No player is permitted to cover more or less permanently the button of his own clock with one of his fingers.

7. During the game the clock must not be picked up by either player.

The Won Game

8. A game is won by the player:

   a. who has mated his opponent's king;

   b. whose opponent resigns;

   c. whose opponent completes an illegal move, which includes leaving his king in check or moving his king into check, but only if the player claims the win before he himself touches a piece (see rule 17) or if he captures that king as valid proof; or

   d. whose opponent's flag falls first, at any time before the game is otherwise ended.

9. A player must claim a win himself by immediately stopping both clocks and notifying the arbiter. To claim

a win under rule 8.d., the player's flag must be up and his opponent's flag must be down after the clocks have been stopped.

If both flags are down, the game is declared a draw—see rule 10.c.

The Drawn Game

10. A game is drawn:

   a. if one of the kings is stalemated;

   b. by agreement between the players during the game, not before or after the game;

   c. if the flag of one player falls after the flag of the other player has already fallen and a win has not been claimed;

   d. if a player demonstrates a perpetual check or a forced repetition of position under the conditions of Article 10.5 of the laws of chess;

   e. if both players have insufficient material for a possible checkmate (only king vs. king, king and bishop vs. king, king and knight vs. king, king and bishop vs. king and bishop on diagonals of the same color); or

   f. if one player has insufficient material for a possible checkmate as described in rule 10.e. and his opponent's flag falls first.

11. The player having the white pieces must notify the arbiter of a drawn game.

Miscellaneous

12. If a player accidentally displaces one or more pieces, he shall replace them on his own time. If it is necessary, his opponent may start the player's clock without making a move in order to make sure that the player replaces the displaced pieces on his own time.

13. Play shall be governed by the FIDE laws of chess and the FIDE interpretations of these laws in all cases to which they apply and in which they are consistent with these rules. In particular, Article 7 ("The Touched Piece") remains in full force. If a player first touches one piece and then moves another, his opponent should restart the player's clock, if it is necessary, and inform him that he must complete the move in accordance with Article 7.

14. In case of a dispute, either player may stop the clocks while the arbiter is being summoned. All of these rules are subject to interpretation by the arbiter, whose decisions are final.

15. Spectators and participants in another game are not to speak or otherwise to interfere in another game. If a spectator interferes in any way, such as by calling attention to a flag fall or an illegal move, the arbiter may cancel the game and rule that a new game be played in its stead, as well as expel the offending party from the playing room. The arbiter, too, must refrain from calling attention to a flag fall or an illegal move, as this is entirely the responsibility of the players themselves.

16. The arbiter shall not handle the clock except in the case of a dispute or when both players ask him to do so.

17. A move is completed as soon as the player's hand has released a piece in accordance with Article 6 of the laws of chess.

18. Illegal moves unnoticed by both players cannot be corrected afterwards, nor can they afterwards lead to a claim of a won game under rule 8.c.

19. Before a five-minute lightning tournament, the organizers should hand out a copy of these rules to each participant, or, if this is not possible, see that a sufficient number of copies of these rules are posted in the playing room at least half an hour before the tournament is to begin.

CHAPTER 16

Round-Robin Pairing Tables

The following pairing tables are used for round-robin tournaments. The player with the first number in each pairing has the white pieces. Pairing numbers are assigned by lot at the beginning of the event, unlike Swiss tournaments in which pairing numbers are determined by ratings.

The advantage of these Crenshaw-Berger tables over other tables is that they reduce the distortion of color assignments in cases when a player withdraws in the first half of a tournament with an even number of players. In such an event, players are already assigned unequal blacks and whites, and the withdrawal of one player could mean, for example, that some competitors would actually play two more blacks than whites.

The Crenshaw system for color equalization minimizes these inequities. The general principles are as follows:

a. If no one withdraws before playing at least half the scheduled games, there are no color changes. ("Half" is always rounded up, so, for example, 6 is half of 11.)

b. If one player withdraws before playing half his games, some colors are reversed in the last rounds.

c. The maximum number of color changes is two for any player.

d. The tournament director may reschedule any games, provided that the games in the starred (*) rounds—those involving color reversals—are played after all players have completed half their games.

Each of the following charts applies to both an odd and an even number of players. If the number of competitors is odd, the final position in the tournament is a bye, but the player scheduled for the bye does not get a scoring point for that round. If there is such a bye in the tournament, no color reversals should be made.

Table A
3 or 4 players

Round	Pairings	
1	1–4	2–3
2	3–1	4–2
3	1–2	3–4

Colors in the third round are determined by toss, unless one player has withdrawn after the first game. In that case, the director assigns colors in the third game so that each remaining player has at least one black and one white in the tournament.

Table B
5 or 6 players

Round	Pairings		
1	3–6	5–4	1–2
2	2–6	4–1	3–5
3	6–5	1–3	3–5
4	6–4	5–1	2–3
5*	1–6	2–5	3–4

*Color reversals should be made in the fifth round if someone withdraws before playing three games:

Withdrawn player	Reversals
1	5–2 4–3
2	4–3
3	none
4	6–1 5–2
5	6–1
6	none

Table C
7 or 8 players

Round	Pairings			
1	4–8	5–3	6–2	7–1
2	8–7	1–6	2–5	3–4
3	3–8	4–2	5–1	6–7
4	8–6	7–5	1–4	2–3
5*	2–8	3–1	4–7	5–6
6*	8–5	6–4	7–3	1–2
7*	1–8	2–7	3–6	4–5

*Color reversals should be made in the last three rounds if someone withdraws before playing four games:

Withdrawn player	Reversals
1	7–2 5–4
2	6–3
3	5–4 7–2 2–1
4	6–3 3–7 7–2
5	8–1 7–4 4–6 6–3
6	8–2 5–4
7	8–1 6–3
8	none

Table D
9 or 10 players

Round	Pairings				
1	5–10	6–4	7–3	8–2	9–1
2	10–9	1–8	2–7	3–6	4–5
3	4–10	5–3	6–2	7–1	8–9
4	10–8	9–7	1–6	2–5	3–4
5	3–10	4–2	5–1	6–9	7–8
6	10–7	8–6	9–5	1–4	2–3
7*	2–10	3–1	4–9	5–8	6–7
8*	10–6	7–5	8–4	9–3	1–2
9*	1–10	2–9	3–8	4–7	5–6

*Color reversals should be made in the last three rounds if someone withdraws before playing five games:

Withdrawn player	*Reversals*
1	9–2 7–4
2	8–3 6–5
3	7–4 9–2 2–1
4	6–5 8–3 3–9 9–2
5	9–2 2–1 7–4 4–8 8–3
6	10–2 8–5 5–7 7–4
7	10–1 6–5 9–4 4–8 8–3
8	10–2 7–4
9	10–1 8–3 6–5
10	none

Table E
11 or 12 players

Round	Pairings					
1	6–12	7–5	8–4	9–3	10–2	11–1
2	12–11	1–10	2–9	3–8	4–7	5–6
3	5–12	6–4	7–3	8–2	9–1	10–11
4	12–10	11–9	1–8	2–7	3–6	4–5
5	4–12	5–3	6–2	7–1	8–11	9–10
6	12–9	10–8	11–7	1–6	2–5	3–4
7	3–12	4–2	5–1	6–11	7–10	8–9
8	12–8	9–7	10–6	11–5	1–4	2–3
9*	2–12	3–1	4–11	5–10	6–9	7–8
10*	12–7	8–6	9–5	10–4	11–3	1–2
11*	1–12	2–11	3–10	4–9	5–8	6–7

*Color reversals should be made in the last three rounds if someone withdraws before playing six games:

Withdrawn player	Reversals
1	11–2 9–4 7–6
2	10–3 8–5
3	9–4 7–6 11–2 2–1
4	8–5 10–3 3–11 11–2
5	7–6 11–2 2–1 9–4 4–10 10–3
6	10–3 3–11 11–2 8–5 5–9 9–4
7	12–1 11–4 4–10 10–3 9–6 6–8 8–5
8	12–2 7–6 10–5 5–9 9–4
9	12–1 8–5 11–4 4–10 10–3
10	12–2 9–4 7–6
11	12–1 10–3 8–5
12	none

Table F
13 or 14 players

Round	Pairings						
1	7–14	8–6	9–5	10–4	11–3	12–2	13–1
2	14–13	1–12	2–11	3–10	4–9	5–8	6–7
3	6–14	7–5	8–4	9–3	10–2	11–1	12–13
4	14–12	13–11	1–10	2–9	3–8	4–7	5–6
5	5–14	6–4	7–3	8–2	9–1	10–13	11–12
6	14–11	12–10	13–9	1–8	2–7	3–6	4–5
7	4–14	5–3	6–2	7–1	8–13	9–12	10–11
8	14–10	11–9	12–8	13–7	1–6	2–5	3–4
9	3–14	4–2	5–1	6–13	7–12	8–11	9–10
10	14–9	10–8	11–7	12–6	13–5	1–4	2–3
11*	2–14	3–1	4–13	5–12	6–11	7–10	8–9
12*	14–8	9–7	10–6	11–5	12–4	13–3	1–2
13*	1–14	2–13	3–12	4–11	5–10	6–9	7–8

*Color reversals should be made in the last three rounds if someone withdraws before playing seven games:

Withdrawn player	Reversals
1	13–2 11–4 9–6
2	12–3 10–5 8–7
3	13–2 2–1 11–4 9–6
4	12–3 3–13 13–2 10–5 8–7
5	13–2 2–1 11–4 4–12 12–3 9–6
6	12–3 3–13 13–2 10–5 5–11 11–4 8–7
7	13–2 2–1 11–4 4–12 12–3 9–6 6–10 10–5
8	14–2 12–5 5–11 11–4 10–7 7–9 9–6
9	14–1 13–4 4–12 12–3 11–6 6–10 10–5 8–7

Table F *(continued)*

Withdrawn player	Reversals
10	14–2 12–5 5–11 11–4 9–6
11	14–1 13–4 4–12 12–3 10–5 8–7
12	14–2 11–4 9–6
13	14–1 12–3 10–5 8–7
14	none

Table G
15 or 16 players

Round	Pairings							
1	8–16	9–7	10–6	11–5	12–4	13–3	14–2	15–1
2	16–15	1–14	2–13	3–12	4–11	5–10	6–9	7–8
3	7–16	8–6	9–5	10–4	11–3	12–2	13–1	14–15
4	16–14	15–13	1–12	2–11	3–10	4–9	5–8	6–7
5	6–16	7–5	8–4	9–3	10–2	11–1	12–15	13–14
6	16–13	14–12	15–11	1–10	2–9	3–8	4–7	5–6
7	5–16	6–4	7–3	8–2	9–1	10–15	11–14	12–13
8	16–12	13–11	14–10	15–9	1–8	2–7	3–6	4–5
9	4–16	5–3	6–2	7–1	8–15	9–14	10–13	11–12
10	16–11	12–10	13–9	14–8	15–7	1–6	2–5	3–4
11	3–16	4–2	5–1	6–15	7–14	8–13	9–12	10–11
12	16–10	11–9	12–8	13–7	14–6	15–5	1–4	2–3
13*	2–16	3–1	4–15	5–14	6–13	7–12	8–11	9–10
14*	16–9	10–8	11–7	12–6	13–5	14–4	15–3	1–2
15*	1–16	2–15	3–14	4–13	5–12	6–11	7–10	8–9

*Color reversals should be made in the last three rounds if someone withdraws before playing eight games:

Withdrawn player	Reversals
1	15–2 13–4 11–6 9–8
2	14–3 12–5 10–7
3	13–4 11–6 9–8 15–2 2–1
4	12–5 10–7 14–3 3–15 15–2
5	11–6 9–8 15–2 2–1 13–4 4–14 14–3
6	10–7 14–3 3–15 15–2 12–5 5–13 13–4
7	9–8 15–2 2–1 13–4 4–14 14–3 11–6 6–12 12–5
8	14–3 3–15 15–2 12–5 5–13 13–4 10–7 7–11 11–6
9	16–1 15–4 4–14 14–3 13–6 6–12 12–5 11–8 8–10 10–7
10	16–2 9–8 14–5 5–13 13–4 12–7 7–11 11–6
11	16–1 10–7 15–4 4–14 14–3 13–6 6–12 12–5
12	16–2 11–6 9–8 14–5 5–13 13–4
13	16–1 12–5 10–7 15–4 4–14 14–3
14	16–2 13–4 11–6 9–8
15	16–1 14–3 12–5 10–7
16	none

Table H
17 or 18 players

Round				Pairings				
1	9–18	10–8	11–7	12–6	13–5	14–4	15–3	16–2	17–1
2	18–17	1–16	2–15	3–14	4–13	5–12	6–11	7–10	8–9
3	8–18	9–7	10–6	11–5	12–4	13–3	14–2	15–1	16–17
4	18–16	17–15	1–14	2–13	3–12	4–11	5–10	6–9	7–8
5	7–18	8–6	9–5	10–4	11–3	12–2	13–1	14–17	15–16
6	18–15	16–14	17–13	1–12	2–11	3–10	4–9	5–8	6–7
7	6–18	7–5	8–4	9–3	10–2	11–1	12–17	13–16	14–15
8	18–14	15–13	16–12	17–11	1–10	2–9	3–8	4–7	5–6
9	5–18	6–4	7–3	8–2	9–1	10–17	11–16	12–15	13–14
10	18–13	14–12	15–11	16–10	17–9	1–8	2–7	3–6	4–5
11	4–18	5–3	6–2	7–1	8–17	9–16	10–15	11–14	12–13
12	18–12	13–11	14–10	15–9	16–8	17–7	1–6	2–5	3–4
13	3–18	4–2	5–1	6–17	7–16	8–15	9–14	10–13	11–12
14	18–11	12–10	13–9	14–8	15–7	16–6	17–5	1–4	2–3
15*	2–18	3–1	4–17	5–16	6–15	7–14	8–13	9–12	10–11
16*	18–10	11–9	12–8	13–7	14–6	15–5	16–4	17–3	1–2
17*	1–18	2–17	3–16	4–15	5–14	6–13	7–12	8–11	9–10

*Color reversals should be made in the last three rounds if someone withdraws before playing nine games:

Withdrawn player	*Reversals*
1	17–2 15–4 13–6 11–8
2	16–3 14–5 12–7 10–9
3	15–4 13–6 11–8 17–2 2–1
4	14–5 12–7 10–9 16–3 3–17 17–2
5	13–6 11–8 17–2 2–1 15–4 4–16 16–3
6	12–7 10–9 16–3 3–17 17–2 14–5 5–15 15–4
7	11–8 17–2 2–1 15–4 4–16 16–3 13–6 6–14 14–5
8	10–9 16–3 3–17 17–2 14–5 5–15 15–4 12–7 7–13 13–6
9	17–2 2–1 15–4 4–16 16–3 13–6 6–14 14–5 11–8 8–12 12–7
10	18–2 16–5 5–15 15–4 14–7 7–13 13–6 12–9 9–11 11–8
11	18–1 10–9 17–4 4–16 16–3 15–6 6–14 14–5 13–8 8–12 12–7
12	18–2 11–8 16–5 5–15 15–4 14–7 7–13 13–6
13	18–1 12–7 10–9 17–4 4–16 16–3 15–6 6–14 14–5
14	18–2 13–6 11–8 16–5 5–15 15–4
15	18–1 14–5 12–7 10–9 17–4 4–16 16–3
16	18–2 15–4 13–6 11–8
17	18–1 16–3 14–5 12–7 10–9
18	none

Table I
19 or 20 players

Round	Pairings									
1	10–20	11–9	12–8	13–7	14–6	15–5	16–4	17–3	18–2	19–1
2	20–19	1–18	2–17	3–16	4–15	5–14	6–13	7–12	8–11	9–10
3	9–20	10–8	11–7	12–6	13–5	14–4	15–3	16–2	17–1	18–19
4	20–18	19–17	1–16	2–15	3–14	4–13	5–12	6–11	7–10	8–9
5	8–20	9–7	10–6	11–5	12–4	13–3	14–2	15–1	16–19	17–18
6	20–17	18–16	19–15	1–14	2–13	3–12	4–11	5–10	6–9	7–8
7	7–20	8–6	9–5	10–4	11–3	12–2	13–1	14–19	15–18	16–17
8	20–16	17–15	18–14	19–13	1–12	2–11	3–10	4–9	5–8	6–7
9	6–20	7–5	8–4	9–3	10–2	11–1	12–19	13–18	14–17	15–16
10	20–15	16–14	17–13	18–12	19–11	1–10	2–9	3–8	4–7	5–6
11	5–20	6–4	7–3	8–2	9–1	10–19	11–18	12–17	13–16	14–15
12	20–14	15–13	16–12	17–11	18–10	19–9	1–8	2–7	3–6	4–5
13	4–20	5–3	6–2	7–1	8–19	9–18	10–17	11–16	12–15	13–14
14	20–13	14–12	15–11	16–10	17–9	18–8	19–7	1–6	2–5	3–4
15	3–20	4–2	5–1	6–19	7–18	8–17	9–16	10–15	11–14	12–13
16	20–12	13–11	14–10	15–9	16–8	17–7	18–6	19–5	1–4	2–3
17*	2–20	3–1	4–19	5–18	6–17	7–16	8–15	9–14	10–13	11–12
18*	20–11	12–10	13–9	14–8	15–7	16–6	17–5	18–4	19–3	1–2
19*	1–20	2–19	3–18	4–17	5–16	6–15	7–14	8–13	9–12	10–11

*Color reversals should be made in the last three rounds if someone withdraws before playing 10 games:

Withdrawn player	Reversals
1	19–2 17–4 15–6 13–8 11–10
2	18–3 16–5 14–7 12–9
3	17–4 15–6 13–8 11–10 19–2 2–1
4	16–5 14–7 12–9 18–3 3–19 19–2
5	15–6 13–8 11–10 19–2 2–1 17–4 4–18 18–3
6	14–7 12–9 18–3 3–19 19–2 16–5 5–17 17–4
7	13–8 11–10 19–2 2–1 17–4 4–18 18–3 15–6 6–16 16–5
8	12–9 18–3 3–19 19–2 16–5 5–17 17–4 14–7 7–15 15–6
9	11–10 19–2 2–1 17–4 4–18 18–3 15–6 6–16 16–5 13–8 8–14 14–7
10	18–3 3–19 19–2 16–5 5–17 17–4 14–7 7–15 15–6 12–9 9–13 13–8
11	20–1 19–4 4–18 18–3 17–6 6–16 16–5 15–8 8–14 14–7 13–10 10–12 12–9
12	20–2 11–10 18–5 5–17 17–4 16–7 7–15 15–6 14–9 9–13 13–8
13	20–1 12–9 19–4 4–18 18–3 17–6 6–16 16–5 15–8 8–14 14–7

Withdrawn player	Reversals
14	20–2 13–8 11–10 18–5 5–17 17–4 16–7
	7–15 15–6
15	20–1 14–7 12–9 19–4 4–18 18–3 17–6
	6–16 16–5
16	20–2 15–6 13–8 11–10 18–5 5–17 17–4
17	20–1 16–5 14–7 12–9 19–4 4–18 18–3
18	20–2 17–4 15–6 13–8 11–10
19	20–1 18–3 16–5 14–7 12–9
20	none

Table J
21 or 22 players

Round	Pairings									
1	11–22	12–10	13–9	14–8	15–7	16–6	17–5	18–4	19–3	20–2 21–1
2	22–21	1–20	2–19	3–18	4–17	5–16	6–15	7–14	8–13	9–12 10–11
3	10–22	11–9	12–8	13–7	14–6	15–5	16–4	17–3	18–2	19–1 20–21
4	22–20	21–19	1–18	2–17	3–16	4–15	5–14	6–13	7–12	8–11 9–10
5	9–22	10–8	11–7	12–6	13–5	14–4	15–3	16–2	17–1	18–21 19–20
6	22–19	20–18	21–17	1–16	2–15	3–14	4–13	5–12	6–11	7–10 8–9
7	8–22	9–7	10–6	11–5	12–4	13–3	14–2	15–1	16–21	17–20 18–19
8	22–18	19–17	20–16	21–15	1–14	2–13	3–12	4–11	5–10	6–9 7–8
9	7–22	8–6	9–5	10–4	11–3	12–2	13–1	14–21	15–20	16–19 17–18
10	22–17	18–16	19–15	20–14	21–13	1–12	2–11	3–10	4–9	5–8 6–7
11	6–22	7–5	8–4	9–3	10–2	11–1	12–21	13–20	14–19	15–18 16–17
12	22–16	17–15	18–14	19–13	20–12	21–11	1–10	2–9	3–8	4–7 5–6
13	5–22	6–4	7–3	8–2	9–1	10–21	11–20	12–19	13–18	14–17 15–16
14	22–15	16–14	17–13	18–12	19–11	20–10	21–9	1–8	2–7	3–6 4–5
15	4–22	5–3	6–2	7–1	8–21	9–20	10–19	11–18	12–17	13–16 14–15
16	22–14	15–13	16–12	17–11	18–10	19–9	20–8	21–7	1–6	2–5 3–4
17	3–22	4–2	5–1	6–21	7–20	8–19	9–18	10–17	11–16	12–15 13–14
18	22–13	14–12	15–11	16–10	17–9	18–8	19–7	20–6	21–5	1–4 2–3
19*	2–22	3–1	4–21	5–20	6–19	7–18	8–17	9–16	10–15	11–14 12–13
20*	22–12	13–11	14–10	15–9	16–8	17–7	18–6	19–5	20–4	21–3 1–2
21*	1–22	2–21	3–20	4–19	5–18	6–17	7–16	8–15	9–14	10–13 11–12

*Color reversals should be made in the last three rounds if someone withdraws before playing 11 games:

Withdrawn player	Reversals
1	12–2 19–4 17–6 15–8 13–10
2	20–3 18–5 16–7 14–9 12–11
3	19–4 17–6 15–8 13–10 21–2 2–1
4	18–5 16–7 14–9 12–11 20–3 3–21 21–2
5	17–6 15–8 13–10 21–2 2–1 19–4 4–20
	20–3

Table J *(continued)*

Withdrawn player	Reversals
6	16–7 14–9 12–11 20–3 3–21 21–2 18–5 5–19 19–4
7	15–8 13–10 21–2 2–1 19–4 4–20 20–3 17–6 6–18 18–5
8	14–9 12–11 20–3 3–21 21–2 18–5 5–19 19–4 16–7 7–17 17–6
9	13–10 21–2 2–1 19–4 4–20 20–3 17–6 6–18 18–5 15–8 8–16 16–7
10	12–11 20–3 3–21 21–2 18–5 5–19 19–4 16–7 7–17 17–6 14–9 9–15 15–8
11	21–2 2–1 19–4 4–20 20–3 17–6 6–18 18–5 15–8 8–16 16–7 13–10 10–14 14–9
12	22–2 20–5 5–19 19–4 18–7 7–17 17–6 16–9 9–15 15–8 14–11 11–13 13–10
13	22–1 12–11 21–4 4–20 20–3 19–6 6–18 18–5 17–8 8–16 16–7 15–10 10–14 14–9
14	22–2 13–10 20–5 5–19 19–4 18–7 7–17 17–6 16–9 9–15 15–8
15	22–1 14–9 12–11 21–4 4–20 20–3 19–6 6–18 18–5 17–8 8–16 16–7
16	22–2 15–8 13–10 20–5 5–19 19–4 18–7 7–17 17–6
17	22–1 16–7 14–9 12–11 21–4 4–20 20–3 19–6 6–18 18–5
18	22–2 17–6 15–8 13–10 20–5 5–19 19–4
19	22–1 18–5 16–7 14–9 12–11 21–4 4–20 20–3
20	22–2 19–4 17–6 15–8 13–10
21	22–1 20–3 18–5 16–7 14–9 12–11
22	none

Table K
23 or 24 players

Round	Pairings										
1	12–24	13–11	14–10	15–9	16–8	17–7	18–6	19–5	20–4	21–3	22–2	23–1
2	24–23	1–22	2–21	3–20	4–19	5–18	6–17	7–16	8–15	9–14	10–13	11–12
3	11–24	12–10	13–9	14–8	15–7	16–6	17–5	18–4	19–3	20–2	21–1	22–23
4	24–22	23–21	1–20	2–19	3–18	4–17	5–16	6–15	7–14	8–13	9–12	10–11
5	10–24	11–9	12–8	13–7	14–6	15–5	16–4	17–3	18–2	19–1	20–23	21–22
6	24–21	22–20	23–19	1–18	2–17	3–16	4–15	5–14	6–13	7–12	8–11	9–10
7	9–24	10–8	11–7	12–6	13–5	14–4	15–3	16–2	17–1	18–23	19–22	20–21
8	24–20	21–19	22–18	23–17	1–16	2–15	3–14	4–13	5–12	6–11	7–10	8–9
9	8–24	9–7	10–6	11–5	12–4	13–3	14–2	15–1	16–23	17–22	18–21	19–20
10	24–19	20–18	21–17	22–16	23–15	1–14	2–13	3–12	4–11	5–10	6–9	7–8
11	7–24	8–6	9–5	10–4	11–3	12–2	13–1	14–23	15–22	16–21	17–20	18–19
12	24–18	19–17	20–16	21–15	22–14	23–13	1–12	2–11	3–10	4–9	5–8	6–7
13	6–24	7–5	8–4	9–3	10–2	11–1	12–23	13–22	14–21	15–20	16–19	17–18
14	24–17	18–16	19–15	20–14	21–13	22–12	23–11	1–10	2–9	3–8	4–7	5–6
15	5–24	6–4	7–3	8–2	9–1	10–23	11–22	12–21	13–20	14–19	15–18	16–17
16	24–16	17–15	18–14	19–13	20–12	21–11	22–10	23–9	1–8	2–7	3–6	4–5
17	4–24	5–3	6–2	7–1	8–23	9–22	10–21	11–20	12–19	13–18	14–17	15–16
18	24–15	16–14	17–13	18–12	19–11	20–10	21–9	22–8	23–7	1–6	2–5	3–4
19	3–24	4–2	5–1	6–23	7–22	8–21	9–20	10–19	11–18	12–17	13–16	14–15
20	24–14	15–13	16–12	17–11	18–10	19–9	20–8	21–7	22–6	23–5	1–4	2–3
21*	2–24	3–1	4–23	5–22	6–21	7–20	8–19	9–18	10–17	11–16	12–15	13–14
22*	24–13	14–12	15–11	16–10	17–9	18–8	19–7	20–6	21–5	22–4	23–3	1–2
23*	1–24	2–23	3–22	4–21	5–20	6–19	7–18	8–17	9–16	10–15	11–14	12–13

*Color reversals should be made in the last three rounds if someone withdraws before playing 12 games:

Withdrawn player	Reversals
1	23–2 21–4 19–6 17–8 15–10 13–12
2	22–3 20–5 18–7 16–9 14–11
3	21–4 19–6 17–8 15–10 13–12 23–2 2–1
4	20–5 18–7 16–9 14–11 22–3 3–23 23–2
5	19–6 17–8 15–10 13–12 23–2 2–1 21–4 4–22 22–3
6	18–7 16–9 14–11 22–3 3–23 23–2 20–5 5–21 21–4
7	17–8 15–10 13–12 23–2 2–1 21–4 4–22 22–3 19–6 6–20 20–5
8	16–9 14–11 22–3 3–23 23–2 20–5 5–21 21–4 18–7 7–19 19–6
9	15–10 13–12 23–2 2–1 21–4 4–22 22–3 19–6 6–20 20–5 17–8 8–18 18–7
10	14–11 22–3 3–23 23–2 20–5 5–21 21–4 18–7 7–19 19–6 16–9 9–17 17–8
11	13–12 23–2 2–1 21–4 4–22 22–3 19–6 6–20 20–5 17–8 8–18 18–7 15–10 10–16 16–9

Table K *(continued)*

Withdrawn player	Reversals
12	22–3 3–23 23–2 20–5 5–21 21–4 18–7 7–19 19–6 16–9 9–17 17–8 14–11 11–15 15–10
13	24–1 23–4 4–22 22–3 21–6 6–20 20–5 19–8 8–18 18–7 17–10 10–16 16–9 15–12 12–14 14–11
14	24–2 13–12 22–5 5–21 21–4 20–7 7–19 19–6 18–9 9–17 17–8 16–11 11–15 15–10
15	24–1 14–11 23–4 4–22 22–3 21–6 6–20 20–5 19–8 8–18 18–7 17–10 10–16 16–9
16	24–2 15–10 13–12 22–5 5–21 21–4 20–7 7–19 19–6 18–9 9–17 17–8
17	24–1 16–9 14–11 23–4 4–22 22–3 21–6 6–20 20–5 19–8 8–18 18–7
18	24–2 17–8 15–10 13–12 22–5 5–21 21–4 20–7 7–19 19–6
19	24–1 18–7 16–9 14–11 23–4 4–22 22–3 21–6 6–20 20–5
20	24–2 19–6 17–8 15–10 13–12 22–5 5–21 21–4
21	24–1 20–5 18–7 16–9 14–11 23–4 4–22 22–3
22	24–2 21–4 19–6 17–8 15–10 13–12
23	24–1 22–3 20–5 18–7 16–9 14–11
24	none

CHAPTER 17

The Scheveningen System

The Scheveningen System is for team matches. The idea is that each member of a team contests a game with each member of the other team.

Pairing tables follow, with the teams called A and B, board numbers indicated by the subscript, and the white player indicated first in each pairing.

TABLES FOR THE SCHEVENINGEN SYSTEM

Match on 4 boards

Round 1	Round 2	Round 3	Round 4
A_1-B_1	B_2-A_1	A_1-B_3	B_4-A_1
A_2-B_2	B_1-A_2	A_2-B_4	B_3-A_2
B_3-A_3	A_3-B_4	B_1-A_3	A_3-B_2
B_4-A_4	A_4-B_3	B_2-A_4	A_4-B_1

Match on 6 boards

Round 1	Round 2	Round 3	Round 4	Round 5	Round 6
B_1-A_1	B_2-A_1	A_1-B_3	A_1-B_4	B_5-A_1	A_1-B_6
B_5-A_2	A_2-B_1	A_2-B_2	B_6-A_2	B_4-A_2	A_2-B_3
A_3-B_4	B_3-A_3	B_1-A_3	A_3-B_5	A_3-B_6	B_2-A_3
A_4-B_2	B_4-A_4	B_6-A_4	A_4-B_1	B_3-A_4	A_4-B_5
A_5-B_3	A_5-B_6	B_5-A_5	B_2-A_5	A_5-B_1	B_4-A_5
B_6-A_6	A_6-B_5	A_6-B_4	B_3-A_6	A_6-B_2	B_1-A_6

Match on 8 boards

Round 1	Round 2	Round 3	Round 4	Round 5	Round 6	Round 7	Round 8
A_1-B_1	B_2-A_1	A_1-B_3	B_4-A_1	A_1-B_5	B_6-A_1	A_1-B_7	B_8-A_1
A_2-B_2	B_3-A_2	A_2-B_4	B_1-A_2	A_2-B_6	B_7-A_2	A_2-B_8	B_5-A_2
A_3-B_3	B_4-A_3	A_3-B_1	B_2-A_3	A_3-B_7	B_8-A_3	A_3-B_5	B_6-A_3
A_4-B_4	B_1-A_4	A_4-B_2	B_3-A_4	A_4-B_8	B_5-A_4	A_4-B_6	B_7-A_4
B_5-A_5	A_5-B_6	B_7-A_5	A_5-B_8	B_1-A_5	A_5-B_2	B_3-A_5	A_5-B_4
B_6-A_6	A_6-B_7	B_8-A_6	A_6-B_5	B_2-A_6	A_6-B_3	B_4-A_6	A_6-B_1
B_7-A_7	A_7-B_8	B_5-A_7	A_7-B_6	B_3-A_7	A_7-B_4	B_1-A_7	A_7-B_2
B_8-A_8	A_8-B_5	B_6-A_8	A_8-B_7	B_4-A_8	A_8-B_1	B_2-A_8	A_8-B_3

CHAPTER 18

About the United States Chess Federation

186 Route 9W
New Windsor, NY 12550
(914) 562-8350

The United States Chess Federation is the official U.S. organization for chess players and chess supporters of all strengths, from beginners to Grandmasters. U.S. Chess represents America in the World Chess Federation, linking U.S. members to chess players around the world. U.S. Chess members are America's chess people of all ages.

Individual Membership

Members of USCF are entitled to the following benefits, among others:

- *Chess Life* magazine—the internationally famous, full-color magazine for chess players. Stories about famous players, great games, photos, and chess lessons—every month.
- Low group rates on many important kinds of personal insurance.

- The opportunity to play chess by mail and meet new chess friends across town or across the U.S.
- Information about clubs and tournaments all over the country.
- Measurement of skill improvement with the U.S. Chess rating system, which is now adopted worldwide.
- Discounts and advice on chess books and equipment.

Affiliation

U.S. Chess Federation affiliates form a team of over 1,300 chess clubs nationwide that supports chess in the U.S. These affiliates are the cornerstone of growth for chess in our country. Any group of chess players may affiliate with USCF at a small annual fee. The benefits include the following:

- The right to sponsor officially rated tournaments.
- Commissions on certain types of membership dues collected.
- Special discounts on chess books and equipment.
- A monthly copy of *Chess Life*.
- The U.S. Chess Federation rating list and supplements, which update members' ratings based on their play in recent events.
- The right to announce their tournaments in *Chess Life* and a substantial discount on *Chess Life* display advertising for their tournaments.
- Free promotional pamphlets and materials (on request) for use in local promotions.

INDEX